THE SPROUTER'S COOKBOOK

by Marjorie Blanchard

ILLUSTRATED BY *Carole Schaetz*

GARDEN WAY PUBLISHING

CHARLOTTE, VERMONT

Library of Congress Catalog Card Number: 74–83147
ISBN 0–88266–041–1 paper
ISBN 0–88266–042–x casebound

Copyright 1975 by Garden Way Publishing Co.
Charlotte, Vermont 05445

Printed in the United States

Second Printing, September, 1975

THE SPROUTER'S COOKBOOK

CONTENTS

INTRODUCTION

Sprouting is a many-faceted activity whose devotees range widely in age and occupation. Children sprout seeds in school to learn at first-hand the miracle of growth; college students have sprouting trays in their rooms to provide them with healthier and more economical sources of food; the knowledgeable nutritionist finds sprouts are the answer to chemical additives; a concerned mother alleviates menu boredom and gives her family extra protein and vitamins by adding sprouts subtly to everyday meals; and the condominium dweller tends an easy-care garden on his kitchen counter with a minimum outlay and a maximum return on an investment of a few jars and some seeds.

As we go into a period of worldwide concern about the most basic necessity to human survival—food—we are more aware than ever of the importance of stretching a little into a lot, of virtually making something out of nothing. A challenging subject becomes an absorbing occupation to anyone interested in our food economy. After a period of great affluence we are getting back to basics, and sprouting seeds for food has been basic throughout the history of mankind.

Sprouting can become a household habit, whether we try it for nutrition, occupational therapy or economy. The wide variety of seeds that can be sprouted add a great variety of flavors to our usual foods. And although we seem to shy away from something that is "good for us," sprouts are. Give your children a souffléd oven pancake for breakfast; it will stay hunger pangs until lunch. Winter salads have summer's crunch when sparked with crispy lentils or mung beans. A nonfattening and delicious dinner can be built around crêpes made from alfalfa sprouts.

This book is intended to add sophistication to the simple sprout, to add a new dimension to your ordinary meal planning, and to show that an ancient ritual can become part of a modern housewife's daily activities.

SPROUTS MAKE SENSE

This book was written in answer to a simple question asked by an average housewife: "I think sprouting is fun, but then what do I do with them? I've tried the salad bit."

Before answering her question specifically, let's begin at the very beginning and first establish exactly what sprouts are. Then we can discuss why they are important to daily life, diet, activities and budget.

Sprouts are seeds of grains or legumes that have germinated and converted their fats and starches into vitamins, sugars and proteins. Any viable seed can be sprouted under the proper conditions, but some are more palatable than others; some have more varied uses; some started out as cattle fodder and should remain there; some will add new tastes and textures to your meals and a spark to your menus that may be lacking.

WHY SPROUT

Our number one concern these days is our health (and rightfully so), as we are deluged from all sides by nutritionists, doctors and health authorities advising us that the American way of eating, which has sustained us these many years in affluent fashion, is mostly, if not all, wrong. Our diet of poptarts and hamburgers will lead to serious medical problems as well as obesity. Woe be unto him who lives on fast foods with additives.

But except by producing everything we eat in our own backyards, where do we go for healthy, untainted foods? We go back into history a bit and like good students we learn from those who have gone before.

Sprouted seeds are a basic source of life and have been a major nutrition factor for many thousands of years, the earliest recorded mention in 2939 B.C. in China.

It is said that a Chinaman lived 257 years "in good repair" on a diet of grains, fruit and sprouts. This is touting sprouts as a miracle food which they are not, but they are a prime source of nutrients and have high food potency.

A seed is made up of the embryo and the endosperm, which is stored carbohydrates, oils and protein. Before a seed is sprouted it is full of fats and starches, but when it germinates under the right conditions and is harvested at the right moment, these fats and starches are changed into vitamins, sugars and protein. Therefore, this sprouted seed, grain or bean is more digestible, less fattening and more nutritious than it was before. In oats, for instance, that have been sprouted for five days, there is a 500% increase in B6, 600% increase in folic acid, 10% increase in B1 and a 1350% increase in B2. Because the starch has been converted to sugar, the sprouts are quickly and easily assimilated by the body and produce the quick energy which we all seem to need in unlimited amounts these days.

Sprouts are not wonder drugs. They are just natural additives which will increase the nutritional value of your daily diet. Many medical people are concluding that food can be our best medicine—that an apple a day will keep the pills away. The research done on sprouts, some of it on history's battlefields, reads like a lot of blue-sky claims, with cures for scurvy and beri-beri leading the pack. Generally speaking, this does not impress most of us, for these are not problems we will have to face. Our main concern is feeling well every day, avoiding minor health worries and keeping our bodies running along without breakdowns. If there are ways to further this that are easy, more economical and even entertaining, let's try it. It can't hurt and it will surely help.

While we are a protein-eating nation brought up on meat, we will have to change our basic food pattern to meet the exigencies of a starving world around us. It will be largely a matter of cutting down rather than cutting out, as we revise our eating habits.

Feeding the world is going to cost somebody money, and it obviously will be the wealthier countries which shoulder the financial responsibility. The moving finger points to the food-rich United States, where most of us already are feeling the pinch. We are being told to tighten the belt as we tighten the purse strings, while all the old adages about thrift are being dusted off.

How can we stretch what we have and still have as much? That calls for a sleight of hand that the average housewife, accustomed to pre-prepared foods and plates piled high with the best, is not used to performing. Here is where the sprouted seed comes into its own, after 3000 years becoming viable again.

Instead of driving to the supermarket and purchasing a vegetable, fresh, canned or frozen, for which you pay the costs for growing, transportation, processing, storage and markups, you reach into the pantry shelf for a bag of seeds which cost you comparatively little and which will produce much more food value ounce for ounce.

Test this statement by taking the Tion recipe and making it twice. Make it first with crisp, freshly sprouted mung beans. Then do it again with winter-bought zucchini, a little limp, quite tasteless and expensive. The mung beans are not simply a winter vegetable substitute, they are a totally new, fresh vegetable that you have grown in your winter kitchen.

And this leads to the next reason for sprouting seeds: to grow something edible in a small space with a minimum of effort and upkeep. Seed sprouting is a wonderful occupation for the frustrated gardener; frustrated because he is a winter shut-in or because he just doesn't have the land to use for a regular garden. You are actually planting, growing and harvesting food in a small area with very little equipment. It can be done satisfactorily in a small mobile home with two quart jars and a square of screening. This is really non-seasonal vegetable gardening that can be done easily even by the non-gardener.

A seed will grow under almost any conditions—in fact the early Christians planted lentil seeds in the darkest Catacombs on Ash Wednesday and they grew to a height of six inches by Maundy Thursday. There is no need for green thumb talk here, but this cannot be a garden of neglect. The sprouts *do* need rinsing three or four times a day, even if you have to take them to the office with you.

Sprouting really is instant gardening which produces fresh food every day if you schedule it right. No trips to the local hardware store are needed for lots of equipment; you probably have the necessary containers in the house to start right away.

It is increasingly difficult to cut down everywhere *except* on what we eat. So we need supplements especially to make basic proteins go farther. Yet the packaged "stretchers" are expensive, generally tasteless and add little but bulk. In contrast, a handful of sprouted seeds provides fresh-grown, unprocessed, unpoisoned, natural food that greatly increases nutritional values.

Observing at least one meatless day a week may be necessary to hold the budget together. Then a vegetable course can become a full-time entrée if it is Eggplant Racioppi (heavy on the cheese and lentils, full of vitamin B and iron), and supplemented by a good salad, Syrian bread and a fruit dessert. This kind of meal may also teach us to eat less, which would hurt few of us Americans, who could do with a lot less "American Fried."

It is useful to figure out the small ways which do save money and that add up to larger savings in the overall picture. Take a recipe such as the Graham Cake Roll, for instance, and add up the cost of using purchased walnuts or pecans instead of sprouted alfalfa. There is quite a difference in pennies.

We all like things to taste good, too, and insisting it's "good for you" doesn't sell very well, especially to a generation used to even their medicine being candy-coated. Sulphur and molasses tonic died with the Puritan ethic, and even if we knew that a diet of alfalfa would cure our ills, we'd take a chance on something that tasted better.

So give thought to taste and texture when using your sprouts in recipes. Don't make them so obvious that at every meal they bring comments and exclamations that show a bit of underlying suspicion. Incorporate them easily into recipes, using each sprout as a separate entity and considering its specific use for the particular method of preparation. Tossing a handful of sprouts into a salad will go over once for novelty, but no family wants that many surprises in every meal. A sprout should stand on its own in taste and texture, complementing the carrot cake, chicken breasts or corn soufflé.

To sum up, sprouts are a prime source of food that easily can become an important asset to your most creative cooking. They are not a far-out fad for the commune inhabitant or Chinese food enthusiast. They can be as American as apple pie and meat loaf—and a distinct asset to both.

HOW TO SPROUT SEEDS

The most important word for seeds is "viable." They must be fresh and untreated with chemicals. Thanks to the wave of interest in organic gardening, it is comparatively easy to buy sproutable seeds. All health food stores carry some kinds and probably the easiest and most economical way to get them is by mailorder from one of the large natural food sources. (See source list at end of the book.) Seeds keep indefinitely and can be stored on the pantry shelf in jars. As long as they are dry and air-tight they will maintain their viability for years.

This book contains recipes for various types of sprouts that we like best. Some will appeal to you; others may not. You have to do your own experimenting, but probably will find there are six or seven most versatile sprouts with flavors and textures that can be incorporated into any number of dishes with favorable results. Coincidentally, these are also the seeds with the highest food potency, such as soybeans, lentils, garbanzo beans, triticale and alfalfa, which all are high in protein.

Sprouts don't grow well at room temperatures much above 80°, but high humidity is even more of a deterrent.

BASIC METHOD FOR FIRST TRY

EQUIPMENT: 2 wide-mouth glass jars, each at least 2 cup capacity
2 pieces of screening (aluminum, plastic or nylon) to fit jar openings
wire ring to hold screen in place
½ cup mung beans

Wash beans in strainer and pick over to remove broken seeds. Put beans in one jar and fill with four times the amount of water. Let soak overnight. The beans will double in bulk. Place screen and wire rim over jar opening. Drain water off beans.

Put half of beans into other jar with screen top.

Rinse both sets of beans with fresh, cool water.

Do not leave any water in container. Seeds should be damp, not soaked.

Lay jars on their sides in a dark place, not direct sunlight. A corner of the kitchen counter will do.

Good ventilation is important.

Rinse with cool water, pouring it completely out, two or three times each day.

Sprouts will start to appear on the second day.

Sprouts are ready to use by the third or fourth day.

If not using immediately, refrigerate in covered container.

Mung bean sprouts, for instance, will be useable for three days.

OTHER METHODS   For a large amount of sprouts, use large plastic containers, such as ice cream cartons. It is important to have room enough on the bottom for the seeds to spread out. In this way they get enough air so they won't ferment and become rancid. The seeds should smell fresh. If they don't—and very hot weather can cause rancidity—throw them out and wait for cooler days.

Soak sprouts overnight.

Rinse into a large strainer.

Drain and divide into as many containers as necessary.

Wet and wring out paper towels.

Spread a piece of damp paper toweling over each container of sprouts, laying it right down on the seeds. Remove towel, pour sprouts into a strainer and rinse under faucet 3 or 4 times a day. Drop sprouts back into containers, replacing damp towel each time. If using screened racks, remove damp towel and rinse racks with sprouts on them, then replacing towels.

For mucilaginous seeds such as chia, cress, buckwheat:

Use an unglazed clay flower pot saucer.

Thoroughly soak saucer and wipe off.

Measure into it an equal amount of seeds and water.

Let stand until water is absorbed.

Place saucer in dish of water, up to overlapping rim.

Cover seeds with plate over top of saucer.

Seeds will absorb enough moisture through the unglazed saucer to sprout if water is kept at the same level.

When they start to sprout, remove top covering and expose seeds to sunlight so the leaves will absorb chlorophyll.

Small seeds such as cress or radish may be sprouted in a strainer or on a sponge or paper towels. These seeds, because of their size, cannot be rinsed. They must be dampened frequently, but never soaked.

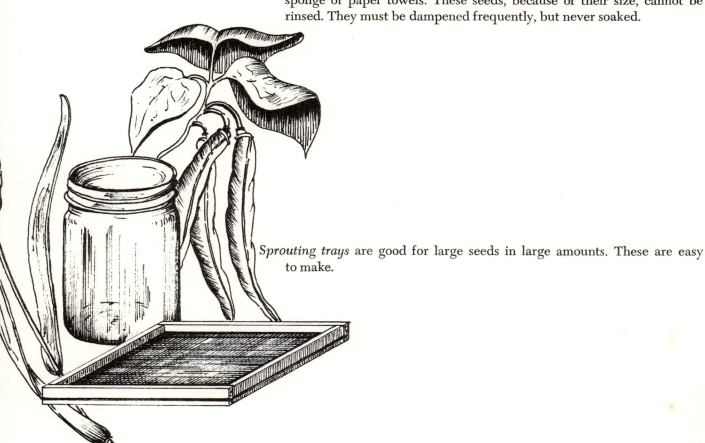

Sprouting trays are good for large seeds in large amounts. These are easy to make.

The method is basically the same. Presoak overnight. Rinse. Spread the seeds on the tray. Cover with a damp paper towel. Place tray on pan to catch drips. Rinse by putting the whole tray under the faucet and shaking to remove excess water. Always replace damp towel. There are also on the market many commercial aids for sprouting.

(*To prepare sprouts to use see under Soybeans.*)

MUNG BEAN

Let's start with the mung bean because it is probably the easiest to sprout, has a crunchy fresh pea flavor and adds zip to other foods, as well as being good to eat on its own. Not all sprouts are. Rich in choline, vitamins A, E and C, the little bright green mung makes an attractive base for baked fish filets, gives crispness to an easy corn timbale and sparks a main course dish or rice ring filled with creamed mushrooms.

METHOD: jar or screen
HARVEST: when sprout is ½ to 1 inch
TIME: 3 to 4 days
YIELD: 1 cup makes 4
NOTE: will get bitter if kept too long.

CORN AND CHICKEN
CHOWDER

SERVES 4–5

2 tbsp. butter or margarine
1 small onion, chopped fine
2 stalks celery, chopped fine
2 medium potatoes, peeled and diced in ½-inch squares
3 cups chicken bouillon
   juice of ½ lemon
   salt to taste
½ tsp. paprika
2 cups diced, cooked chicken
1 cup fresh corn kernels or 1 pkg. frozen corn
½ cup sprouted mung beans
1 cup milk
1 cup light cream
2 tbsp. chopped parsley

Heat butter in large saucepan.
Sauté onion and celery for 5 minutes. Add potatoes.
Cook, stirring for 5 minutes.
Add bouillon, lemon juice, salt and paprika.
Bring to boil, reduce heat and simmer, covered, until vegetables are tender.
Add chicken, corn and mung bean sprouts and cook over medium heat for
      15 minutes.
Add milk and cream and bring almost to a boil.
Serve hot with parsley sprinkled on top.

BAKED BEEF AND NOODLES

SERVES 6

1 pkg. frozen chopped spinach cooked and drained
1 cup mung bean sprouts
½ lb. lean chopped chuck
½ cup dry bread crumbs
½ cup grated Parmesan cheese
½ tsp. ground nutmeg
   grated rind of ½ lemon
1 egg

Mix above ingredients all together and set aside.

2 tbsp. chopped shallots
2 tbsp. butter or margarine
4 tbsp flour
2 cups beef bouillon
1 cup milk
   salt to taste
   freshly-ground pepper
8 oz. noodles
1 cup tomato sauce
½ cup chives
½ cup grated Swiss cheese

Preheat oven to 350°.
Heat butter in saucepan and sauté shallots for 5 minutes, stirring.
Stir in flour and cook for 2 minutes.
Add bouillon and milk and cook, stirring, until thickened.
Butter a 2½ qt. casserole.
Layer ingredients as follows: ½ the noodles on bottom, ½ cup tomato sauce, 4 tbsp. chives, ½ meat mixture, ½ white sauce. Repeat ending with white sauce.
Sprinkle grated cheese over top.
Bake for 30 minutes.

FISH EN CASSEROLE

SERVES 6

2 lbs. haddock or cod, in one piece
2 cups sprouted mung beans
½ cup chopped parsley
¼ cup chopped chives
1 tbsp. fresh snipped dill
4 tbsp. butter or margarine
   juice of ½ lemon or 1 lime
   salt to taste
   freshly-ground pepper

Preheat oven to 400°.
Grease bottom of a flat baking dish large enough to hold the fish in one layer.
Mix together the mung beans, parsley, chives and dill.
Spread over bottom of baking dish.
Place fish on top.
Sprinkle with salt, pepper and lemon or lime juice.
Dot with butter.
Place in oven, uncovered, and bake for 20–25 minutes until fish flakes easily
      when fork is inserted into thickest part.
Serve each portion on a bed of the sprouts and herbs.

SHRIMP PILAF

SERVES 6

¼ lb. bacon
1 large onion, chopped
½ medium green pepper, chopped
1 cup regular rice
2¼ cups chicken bouillon
   salt to taste
   freshly-ground pepper
½ tsp. ground ginger or 1 tsp. minced fresh ginger
1 cup mung bean sprouts
1 lb. raw shrimp, peeled and cleaned

In large skillet or saucepan, cook bacon slices until crisp. Drain on paper towels and crumble.
Pour off all but 2 tbsp. fat.
Sauté onion and green pepper in bacon fat until soft, about 10 minutes over medium heat.
Add rice and stir until coated with fat.
Pour in bouillon. Add seasonings.
Cover and cook over medium heat until liquid is absorbed and rice is tender.
Stir in mung beans and shrimp.
Cover and cook 5–7 minutes until shrimp is pink and firm.
Sprinkle bacon over top before serving.

OEUFS TOULONAISE

SERVES 6

3 large tomatoes
2 tbsp. oil
2 tbsp. mung bean sprouts, chopped fine
2 tbsp. chopped parsley
1 tsp. chopped garlic
   salt to taste
   freshly-ground pepper
6 eggs

Slice unpeeled tomatoes into six ½-inch slices.
Heat oil in large skillet.
Fry tomato slices on both sides until hot and soft but not shapeless.
Mix together the chopped sprouts, parsley and garlic.
Sprinkle over the tomato slices.
Season.
Break one egg onto each tomato slice.
Cover and cook until white is firm and yolk is done.

CLAM RISOTTO

SERVES 4

4 tbsp. butter
2 tbsp. chopped shallots or green onion
1 cup regular rice
1 cup clam juice
1 cup water
½ cup dry white wine
  salt to taste
  freshly-ground pepper
½ tsp. thyme
1 8 oz. can minced clams, drained
1 cup mung bean sprouts
2 tbsp. butter

In heavy 2-qt. saucepan heat butter. Add shallots and sauté for 3 minutes. Stir in rice until coated with butter.
Add all liquids and seasonings.
Cover pan and cook over medium heat until liquid has been absorbed, about 20 minutes.
Remove cover and stir in clams and mung bean sprouts.
Let all heat through for 5 minutes.
Add 2 tbsp. butter and serve immediately.
This makes a satisfactory main dish with a green salad and bread, cheese and fruit.

TIAN

SERVES 6

2 medium onions, chopped fine
3 tbsp. butter
1 cup regular rice
2 cups sprouted mung beans
2¼ cups chicken stock or bouillon
  salt to taste
  a lot of freshly-ground pepper
1 cup grated Parmesan cheese

Preheat oven to 325°.
Melt butter in large skillet. Sauté onions over medium heat until soft, about 10 minutes.
Stir in rice and cook until coated, about 3 minutes.
Stir in mung beans and blend with rice and onion.
Transfer mixture to buttered 1½-qt. flat baking dish.
Stir in salt, pepper and cheese.
Pour bouillon over all.
Bake uncovered for 45 minutes until all liquid is absorbed and top is slightly crisp.
NOTE: This casserole freezes well after baking.

OMELET FOR ONE

2 eggs
2 tsp. chopped parsley
2 tsp. chopped chives
2 tbsp. cottage cheese
1 tbsp. mung bean sprouts
    salt to taste
    freshly-ground pepper
2 tsp. butter

Beat eggs in small bowl with fork.
Beat in chopped parsley and chives.
Heat omelet pan until it sizzles when a drop of water is sprinkled on it.
Quickly melt butter in pan.
Pour in egg mixture.
Grasp handle of pan in one hand and fork in other.
Shake pan as you mix the egg with the tines of the fork until egg starts to
    solidify.
Lift up edges of egg and let liquid run underneath.
Omelet is done when underneath part is solid and center is still moist.
Fill center with cottage cheese and sprouts.
Fold over and turn out onto plate.
Season.
Serve immediately.

SAUTÉED GREEN BEANS

SERVES 4

1 lb. green beans, cooked crisp/tender
2 tbsp. butter
1 tbsp. oil
2 tbsp. chopped shallots
¾ cup mung beans sprouts
2 tbsp. chopped parsley
  salt to taste
  freshly-ground pepper
½ tsp. ground nutmeg

In heavy skillet heat butter and oil.
Add shallots and sauté for 3 minutes.
Add sprouts and stir quickly.
Add cooked green beans and quickly toss in butter over high heat, stirring rapidly until vegetable is hot.
Sprinkle with parsley, salt, pepper and nutmeg.
Serve immediately.

ARTICHOKE HEARTS PROVENÇALE

SERVES 4

1 15 oz. can artichoke hearts, packed in brine
2 tbsp. oil
1 clove garlic, crushed
1 cup tomatoes, drained
½ cup mung bean sprouts
½ tsp. oregano
½ tsp. basil
  salt to taste
  freshly-ground pepper
½ cup dry bread crumbs
4 tbsp. grated Parmesan cheese

Preheat oven to 350°.
Drain artichoke hearts and rinse in cold water. Pat dry. Cut in halves.
Heat oil in skillet and sauté garlic briefly. Do not brown.
Add artichoke hearts to skillet and sauté for 5 minutes, stirring.
Remove artichoke hearts to shallow baking dish.
Add to skillet the tomatoes, oregano, basil, salt and pepper.
Simmer for 10 minutes. Stir in sprouts.
Pour over vegetable in baking dish.
Sprinkle with crumbs and cheese.
Bake for 20 minutes.

SPANISH RICE

SERVES 4

1 cup sliced onions
½ cup butter or margarine
½ cup rice
2 cups canned tomatoes, drained through a sieve
1 cup beef bouillon
  salt to taste
  freshly-ground pepper
1 tsp. chili powder
½ cup mung bean sprouts
½ cup grated sharp Cheddar cheese

Preheat oven to 350°.
Heat butter in skillet and sauté onions until limp.
Place in bottom of 1½ qt. casserole.
Spread rice over onions.
Pour tomatoes over rice.
Sprinkle mung bean sprouts over tomatoes.
Pour over bouillon.
Add seasonings.
Sprinkle cheese over top.
Cover and bake for 1 hour.
Uncover and bake 10 minutes longer.
Accompany with cornbread, avocado salad, fruit with custard.

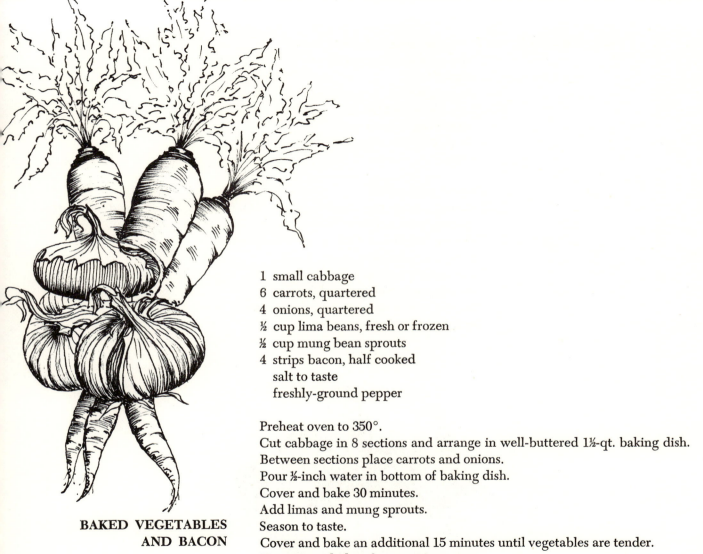

1 small cabbage
6 carrots, quartered
4 onions, quartered
½ cup lima beans, fresh or frozen
½ cup mung bean sprouts
4 strips bacon, half cooked
  salt to taste
  freshly-ground pepper

Preheat oven to 350°.
Cut cabbage in 8 sections and arrange in well-buttered 1½-qt. baking dish.
Between sections place carrots and onions.
Pour ½-inch water in bottom of baking dish.
Cover and bake 30 minutes.
Add limas and mung sprouts.
Season to taste.
Cover and bake an additional 15 minutes until vegetables are tender.
Uncover and place bacon strips on top.
Bake until bacon is done.

**BAKED VEGETABLES
AND BACON**

SERVES 4–5

CORN TIMBALES

SERVES 6

1 cup corn kernels, fresh or frozen
½ cup medium or heavy cream
1 tsp. salt
1 tsp. paprika
1 tsp. Dijon mustard
½ cup mung bean sprouts
4 tbsp. grated Parmesan or Swiss cheese
3 eggs

Preheat oven to 350°.
Put corn, cream and seasonings in blender with sprouts. Blend for 10 sec-
    onds. Pour into bowl and stir in eggs and cheese, mixing well.
Fill well-buttered custard cups with mixture.
Set cups in pan of hot water.
Cover loosely with foil.
Bake for 20–30 minutes until firm.
Turn out onto rounds of sautéed tomatoes or baked eggplant.
Garnish with chopped parsley.

BROCCOLI TART

SERVES 6

1 9-inch pie shell, pre-baked 10 minutes
2 tbsp. butter or margarine
1 medium onion, chopped fine
1 cup mung bean sprouts
1 pkg. frozen chopped broccoli, cooked and well drained
½ cup ricotta cheese
1 cup sour cream
2 eggs
  salt to taste
  freshly-ground pepper
½ tsp. ground nutmeg
½ cup grated Parmesan cheese

Preheat oven to 350°.
Heat butter in skillet and sauté onion until soft.
Stir in mung beans and sauté 5 minutes.
Spread cooked broccoli over bottom of pie shell.
Sprinkle sprouts and onions over broccoli.
Beat together with fork the ricotta, sour cream, eggs and seasonings.
Pour over mixture in pie shell.
Sprinkle Parmesan cheese over top.
Bake for 30 minutes until set.
Let stand 5 minutes before serving.

STUFFED ZUCCHINI

SERVES 6 – 8

4 medium zucchini
1 clove garlic, minced
2 tbsp. parsley, chopped
2 tbsp. chives, chopped
½ tsp. basil
2 tbsp. oil
½ cup regular rice
1½ cups chicken bouillon
½ cup mung bean sprouts
  salt to taste
  freshly-ground pepper

Split zucchinis in half lengthwise. Scoop out seeds. Sprinkle with salt and
    let stand 20 minutes.
Preheat oven to 350°.
Heat oil in skillet.
Sauté briefly the herbs and garlic. Add rice and stir until coated.
Pour in 1 cup chicken bouillon.
Cover and simmer for 15 minutes.
Season.
Stir in mung bean sprouts.
Drain zucchinis and wipe dry.
Fill zucchini halves with rice mixture.
Place in flat baking dish.
Pour ½ cup bouillon in bottom.
Bake uncovered for 30 minutes.

FRESH GREEN SAUCE

YIELD: 1 CUP

¼ cup chopped parsley
2 tbsp. chopped chives
2 tbsp. mung bean sprouts
5 sprigs watercress
6 fresh spinach leaves
1 clove garlic
1 tsp. tarragon or dill
  salt to taste
  freshly-ground pepper
½ cup mayonnaise
2 tbsp. sour cream

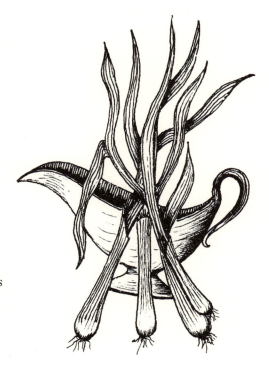

Put all ingredients in blender except sour cream. Blend until smooth.
Pour into bowl and stir in sour cream and seasoning to taste.
Refrigerate for at least 2 hours before using on raw vegetables or cold
    shrimp.

**SAUCE FOR
CAULIFLOWER**

SERVES 4–5

1 head cauliflower, steamed whole
½ pint sour cream
½ tsp. Dijon mustard
   small can deviled ham
2 tbsp. dry bread crumbs
4 tbsp. mung bean sprouts

Put sour cream, mustard, ham and bread crumbs together in saucepan.
Stir gently over medium heat until warm.
Stir in mung bean sprouts.
Pour over cauliflower.

**SAUCE FOR BOILED
NEW POTATOES**

ABOUT 3 CUPS

6 tbsp. butter or margarine
½ lb. mushrooms, sliced
1 clove garlic, crushed
2 tbsp. chopped parsley
2 tbsp. chopped chives
½ cup mung bean sprouts

Heat butter in large skillet. Add garlic and cook over medium heat for 2
   minutes.
Add mushrooms and cook quickly, stirring, for 5 minutes.
Stir in parsley, chives and mung bean sprouts.
Heat through and pour over potatoes.

SALADE NIÇOISE

SERVES 4 – 5

1 7½ oz. can tuna fish, drained
1 cup crisply-cooked green beans in 1-inch lengths
2 medium potatoes, peeled, cooked and diced
3 hardcooked eggs, shelled and quartered
2 large tomatoes, peeled and cut into eighths
½ cup mung bean sprouts
2 flat anchovy fillets, drained
6 pitted black olives (optional)
1 cup mayonnaise
  juice of 1 lemon
  salt to taste
  freshly-ground pepper

Break tuna fish into bite sized pieces.
Place in the center of a large round platter.
Surround with fresh salad greens.
On the greens, around the tuna, arrange small mounds of beans and potatoes.
Intersperse with egg and tomato pieces.
Sprinkle mung beans over tuna.
Criss-cross anchovy fillets over top.
Garnish with olives.
Mix lemon juice, salt and pepper with mayonnaise.
Serve dressing separately.

AUTUMN SALAD

SERVES 4

1 cup mayonnaise
½ cup sour cream
1 tsp. Dijon mustard
  salt to taste
  freshly-ground pepper
1 cup Swiss cheese cut into ½-inch squares
1 cup ham cut into ½-inch squares
1 large apple, cored and diced
1 cup mung bean sprouts

Mix together the mayonnaise, sour cream, mustard, salt and pepper.
Let stand while preparing rest of ingredients.
Combine cheese, ham, apple and sprouts in bowl.
Pour over dressing and mix all together gently.
Serve on fresh salad greens.

HERB BISCUITS

YIELD: TWELVE
2-INCH BISCUITS

2 cups unbleached white flour
4 tsp. baking powder
1 tsp. salt
4 tbsp. butter or shortening
¼ cup mung bean sprouts
2 tbsp. parsley
2 tbsp. chives
⅔ cup buttermilk

Preheat oven to 425°.
Chop together the mung bean sprouts, parsley and chives.
Put flour into large bowl.
Add baking powder and salt.
With fingertips, blend in butter until it is well mixed with flour.
Stir in chopped herbs and sprouts.
Add buttermilk all at once and mix well until a smooth dough is formed.
Turn out and knead for 2 minutes.
Pat or roll into a flat piece.
Cut out rounds with 2-inch biscuit cutter.
Place biscuits on ungreased baking sheet.
Bake for 15 minutes until risen and browned.
NOTE: These biscuits also may be used as topping for chicken or meat pies.

LENTILS

The lentil has been in our consciousness since Jacob first brewed his mess of pottage for his brother Esau. Incidentally, those were red lentils—not as common today as the brown type. These little sprouted legumes, a staple food in many parts of the world for hundreds of years, are inexpensive and nutritious in that they contain large amounts of vitamin B and iron. Their texture is delightfully crisp when eaten raw, and actually they make an excellent substitute for celery or green pepper in the winter months when both of those vegetables are scarce and high in price. Cooked in an eggplant dish or stewed with tomatoes, the sprouted lentil has a somewhat sweet and nutty flavor.

Lentil soup is good, homely fare when brewed with onions and herbs and combined with some sliced sausages, chunks of ham or high-quality frankfurters. A good and nourishing meal is thick lentil soup, crisp greens, homemade whole wheat bread, fruit and cheese. If you start sprouting your lentils and alfalfa at the same time they will mature simultaneously, and a couple of hours in the kitchen will give you enough soup and bread (refer to Alfalfa bread) for at least two meals. Freeze the surplus against an emergency dinner.

Having started at the beginning with pottage, go on and discover the other potentials of lentils. Bake them with mushrooms for a main course. Roll them into a meat loaf. Combine them with chopped onion, parsley, tomato and a vinaigrette dressing for a cool summer salad. And don't forget that the purpose of sprouting these beans is to decrease the starch content and increase the vitamins.

METHOD: Jar
TIME: 3 to 4 days
LENGTH: ½-inch
YIELD: 1 cup makes 4

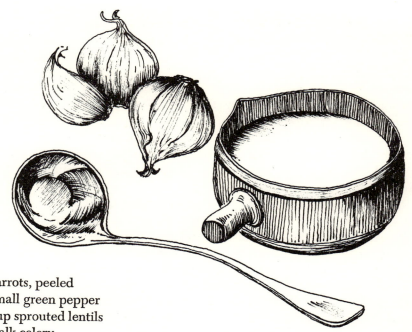

**VEGETABLE SANDWICH
SPREAD**

2 carrots, peeled
1 small green pepper
1 cup sprouted lentils
1 stalk celery
3 radishes
1 8 oz. pkg. cream cheese, softened
  salt to taste
  freshly-ground pepper
  mayonnaise

Put carrots, green pepper, lentils, celery and radishes through fine blade of meat grinder.

Squeeze out excess moisture.

Mix with cream cheese, salt, pepper and enough mayonnaise to make a spreadable mixture.

Use on whole wheat bread or small rolls.

COLD CLAM AND VEGETABLE CONSOMMÉ

SERVES 4

2 cups clam juice
1 cucumber, peeled, seeded and chopped
2 ripe tomatoes, peeled and quartered
2 tbsp. chopped chives
1 tbsp. fresh snipped dill (or 1 tsp. dried)
3–4 celery leaves
½ cup sprouted lentils
   salt to taste
   freshly-ground pepper
2 tsp. chopped parsley

Place all ingredients except salt, pepper and parsley in blender.
Blend until almost smooth.
Season to taste.
Serve chilled garnished with parsley.

LENTIL SOUP

SERVES 4–6

3 tbsp. bacon fat
1 large onion, sliced
2 stalks celery, chopped
1 carrot, peeled and chopped
3 cups sprouted lentils
4 cups water
2 cups chopped tomatoes
  salt to taste
  freshly-ground pepper
½ lb. pre-cooked smoked sausages or frankfurters cut into rounds

In large saucepan or kettle heat bacon fat.
Sauté onion, carrot and celery over medium heat for 10 minutes.
Add lentil sprouts, water, tomatoes and seasonings.
Cover and simmer for 30 minutes.
Put soup into blender and blend until smooth.
Return to kettle and add sausages.
Heat until meat and soup are hot.

HOT POTATO SALAD

SERVES 6

3 lbs. potatoes
½ lb. bacon in ½-inch pieces
½ cup chopped onions
¼ cup vinegar
¼ cup water
½ tsp. salt
   freshly-ground pepper
1 tsp. dry mustard
1 cup sprouted lentils
2 tbsp. chopped chives

Boil potatoes. Drain, peel and cut into ½-inch thick slices. Place in salad
    bowl.
Fry bacon. Remove to drain.
Sauté onions in bacon fat until soft.
Add vinegar, water, salt, pepper and mustard to pan and bring to a boil.
Add lentil sprouts to potato slices in bowl.
Pour hot dressing over all and mix gently.
Sprinkle with bacon bits and chives and serve immediately.

This is a good summer meal with the addition of a cold soup, egg-stuffed
    tomatoes, marinated cucumbers and a sponge cake.

BAKED HAM AND
GREEN NOODLES

SERVES 6

1 8 oz. pkg. green (or spinach) noodles
½ cup cottage cheese
6 tbsp. melted butter
2 egg yolks
1 cup cream, whipped
   salt to taste
   freshly-ground pepper
1 cup chopped ham
1 cup sprouted lentils
1 cup buttered bread crumbs

Preheat oven to 350°.
Cook noodles in boiling salted water until just tender. Drain.
Put cottage cheese, butter and yolks in blender. Blend until smooth.
Combine noodles with egg mixture, whipped cream, salt and pepper.
Butter a 2-qt. baking dish.
Spread lentils on bottom; ham on top of lentils.
Put noodle mixture over all.
Sprinkle with bread crumbs.
Bake for 20 minutes.

MUSHROOM PIE

SERVES 6

1 lb. mushrooms, sliced
1 cup sprouted lentils, steamed
2 shallots, chopped
6 tbsp. butter or margarine
2 tbsp. flour
1½ cups heavy cream
2 egg yolks
1 tsp. ground nutmeg
    salt to taste
    freshly-ground pepper
¼ cup grated Swiss cheese
1 9-inch pie shell, pre-baked 10 minutes

Preheat oven to 375°.
Heat butter in large skillet.
Sauté shallots for 2 minutes over medium heat.
Add mushrooms and sauté, stirring, for 10 minutes, until cooked but not soft.
Sprinkle flour over mushrooms. Cook for 2 minutes.
Beat egg yolks with cream and seasonings.
Add to mushrooms and blend in, stirring until thickened over low heat.
Pour mixture into pie shell.
Sprinkle with cheese.
Bake for 15–20 minutes.

A spinach salad, hot rolls and a lemon dessert complete the meal.

BAKED STUFFED MUSHROOMS

SERVES 4

16 large mushrooms
1 small onion, chopped fine
3 tbsp. butter or margarine
1 cup bread crumbs
1 cup sprouted lentils, chopped
2 tbsp. heavy cream
  salt to taste
  freshly-ground pepper
½ tsp. ground nutmeg
¼ cup grated Parmesan or Swiss cheese

Preheat oven to 375°.
Remove stems from mushrooms and chop them fine.
In heavy skillet, melt 2 tbsp. butter.
Sauté onion until soft.
Add chopped mushroom stems and sauté briefly.
Stir in bread crumbs, lentils and seasonings.
Moisten with cream.
Melt remaining tbsp. butter and brush mushroom caps.
Place caps open side up and fill with lentil-onion mix.
Place in buttered baking dish.
Sprinkle with cheese.
Bake for 15 minutes.

These mushrooms may be served on toast as a main course with a hearty salad and Apple Crisp for dessert.

ROLLED MEAT LOAF

SERVES 6

2 slices whole wheat bread, crusts removed
½ cup milk
½ medium onion, minced
2 lbs. ground chuck
1 tsp. Dijon mustard
2 eggs
  salt to taste
  freshly-ground pepper
2 tbsp. chopped parsley
1 cup sprouted lentils
1 apple, cored, peeled and chopped

Preheat oven to 350°.
Put milk into heavy saucepan. Add onion and bread.
Cover and cook over low heat until onion is soft and bread has dissolved into milk. Mixture will be thick.
Put meat into large bowl.
Add milk mixture, eggs, mustard, salt and pepper. Mix well with hands.
Pat meat mixtures out onto a piece of wax paper into a rectangle approximately 9 x 18 inches.
Spread parsley, lentils and apple over meat.
While removing the wax paper, roll up meat, starting on the long side, into a roll.
Transfer to a 9 x 15-inch baking pan with sides.
Pour ½ cup hot water into bottom of pan.
Bake for 1 hour.
Cut in slices and serve on platter.

FRESH SQUASH
CASSEROLE

SERVES 4

1 lb. yellow summer squash, unpeeled
1 medium onion, chopped
1 cup sprouted lentils
2 eggs
½ cup sour cream
½ cup creamed cottage cheese
   salt to taste
   freshly-ground pepper
⅛ cup grated cheddar cheese
2 tbsp. chopped chives

Preheat oven to 350°.
Grate squash on large holes of grater. Sprinkle with 2 tsp. salt and let stand
   30 minutes. Squeeze dry.
Butter a 1½-qt. baking dish.
Mix together squash, onion and lentils and put into dish.
Beat together eggs, sour cream, cottage cheese, salt and pepper.
Pour over squash.
Sprinkle cheese and chives over top.
Bake for 30 minutes until set and lightly browned.

This could be the main dish for a summer supper with the addition of
   baked tomatoes, herb bread and poached fruit.

EGGPLANT RACIOPPI

SERVES 4

1 large eggplant, unpeeled
4 tbsp. oil
½ cup grated Mozzarella cheese
½ cup grated Romano or Parmesan cheese
2 cups tomato spaghetti sauce
1 cup sprouted lentils
2 eggs
⅔ cup milk
  salt to taste
  freshly-ground pepper

Preheat oven to 375°.
Slice eggplant crosswise into ½-inch slices. Sprinkle each slice with salt and
  let stand ½ hour.
Dry slices.
Heat oil in heavy skillet.
Fry eggplant slices in oil over medium-high heat until lightly browned.
Oil a shallow baking dish that will hold eggplant in two layers.
Put in one layer of eggplant. Pour over 1 cup sauce. Sprinkle with half of
  each kind of cheese. Season.
Spread lentils over cheese.
Cover with rest of eggplant, remaining sauce and cheeses.
Beat eggs and milk together lightly with fork.
Pour over all.
Cover.
Bake for 20–30 minutes until eggs are set.

As eggplant has very little nutritional value, the addition of lentils and
  cheese turns this into a good main dish. Serve with Italian bread, salad
  and a fruit pie.

CELERY AND CARROT CASSEROLE

SERVES 4

1 cup chopped celery
1 cup chopped carrots
½ cup chopped onion
1 cup sprouted lentils
½ cup chopped green pepper
⅛ cup chopped walnuts
2 tbsp. chopped parsley
2 eggs
1 cup milk
  salt to taste
  freshly-ground pepper

Preheat oven to 350°.
Butter a 1½-qt. casserole.
Combine and mix together all vegetables and nuts in casserole.
Beat together the eggs and milk and seasonings.
Pour into casserole.
Set dish in pan of hot water.
Bake 1 hour until set.
Let stand 10 minutes before serving.

This dish is a good accompaniment to ham or chicken.

TURNIPS REMOULADE

SERVES 6

1 lb. white turnips
1 cup mayonnaise
2 tsp. Dijon mustard
½ tsp. dry mustard
1 tbsp. lemon juice
4–6 tbsp. heavy cream
salt to taste
freshly-ground pepper
1 cup sprouted lentils

Peel and cut turnips into julienne strips and put into bowl of cold water.
Combine mayonnaise, mustard and lemon juice in bowl.
Beat together.
Thin to desired consistency with cream.
Season to taste.
Drain and dry turnip strips.
Gently mix turnips and lentils with sauce.
Cover bowl and refrigerate for 1 hour.

SAUTÉED LENTILS

SERVES 4

4 slices bacon
1 onion, chopped
1 cup tomatoes, drained
1 clove garlic, minced
2 cups sprouted lentils
   salt to taste
   freshly-ground pepper
2 tbsp. minced parsley

In large skillet fry bacon until crisp. Remove and drain.
Pour off all but 2 tbsp. bacon fat.
Sauté onion and garlic in fat over medium heat until soft.
Add tomatoes, salt, pepper and parsley.
Simmer, covered, over medium heat for 10 minutes.
Remove cover, stir in lentils and simmer for 10 minutes.
Taste for seasoning.

STEWED TOMATOES

SERVES 4

1 medium onion, chopped
2 tbsp. butter or margarine
1 #2 can tomatoes
2 slices dried whole wheat bread
1 tbsp. brown sugar
½ tsp. thyme
1 tsp. basil or oregano
1 cup sprouted lentils

Heat butter in heavy skillet or saucepan.
Sauté onion over medium heat for 5 minutes.
Pour in tomatoes with liquid.
Crumble bread and stir in.
Add sugar, herbs and seasonings.
Mix in lentils.
Cook over low heat for 1 hour until mixture is thick.

POTATOES IN SOUR CREAM

SERVES 4–5

6 medium potatoes, cooked, peeled, sliced
2 tbsp. butter or margarine
1 clove garlic, minced
½ cup sprouted lentils, chopped
6 tbsp. melted butter
   salt to taste
   freshly-ground pepper
1 cup sour cream
Preheat oven to 350°.

Butter a 1½-qt. baking dish.
Heat butter in skillet and sauté garlic and chopped lentils together for
   5 minutes.
Divide all ingredients in thirds and layer in baking dish as follows: potato
   slices, melted butter, garlic-lentil mixture, salt and pepper, sour cream.
Bake for 30 minutes.

SPINACH RICOTTA

SERVES 6

3 pkg. frozen chopped spinach
½ cup minced onion
2 shallots, chopped
4 tbsp. butter
¼ lb. Feta cheese
1 cup sprouted lentils
3 eggs
½ lb. Ricotta cheese
   salt to taste
   freshly-ground pepper
½ tsp. ground nutmeg
¼ to ½ cup heavy cream
¼ cup grated Parmesan cheese

Preheat oven to 375°.
Cook spinach and drain very dry.
Heat butter in skillet and sauté onion and shallots for 3 minutes.
Add to spinach.
Crumble Feta cheese and mix with spinach.
Beat together eggs and Ricotta cheese.
Mix in lentil sprouts and seasonings.
Combine spinach and lentil mixtures and cream until the consistency is of
    heavy cream sauce.
Pour into a buttered shallow 2-qt. baking dish.
Bake for 30 minutes.

This goes well with ham or pork.

**STUFFED TOMATO
SALAD**

SERVES 4

4 medium tomatoes
¼ cup sprouted lentils
½ cup Swiss cheese, cubed
¼ cup mayonnaise
   salt to taste
   freshly-ground pepper
½ tsp. curry powder

Cut tops off tomatoes. Hollow out. Sprinkle with salt and turn upside down
   to drain for 15 minutes.
Combine lentils, cheese cubes and mayonnaise. Season to taste.
Fill tomatoes with mixture and serve on fresh salad greens.

SUMMER GARDEN SUPPER

SERVES 4

3 large tomatoes, peeled and sliced
2 large onions, thinly sliced
3 medium zucchini, unpeeled and sliced into rounds
1 cup sprouted lentils
1 cup green beans, fresh or frozen, in 1-inch lengths
1 cup fresh or frozen limas
4 tbsp. chopped parsley
2 tbsp. chopped chives
1 clove garlic, chopped
½ cup oil

In a deep, 3- or 4-qt. stove-top casserole place tomato slices on bottom.
Top with onions, then zucchini, then lentils.
Sprinkle over half of parsley, chives, garlic.
Season with salt and pepper to taste.
Put in beans, limas, remaining herbs and garlic.
Season and pour oil over all.
Cover and cook over medium heat for 30 minutes until beans are tender but
     not mushy.

Serve with blueberry muffins and fresh peach pie.

SOYBEANS

Here is the food that the whole world is talking about, for the soybean has become a major interest to all nutritionists and those concerned with feeding the multitudes. And once again it was the Orientals who were making good use of this food source long before the Western world even knew it existed—since 3000 B.C. to be exact. But once we began production on this versatile product, we managed to put it into everything from linoleum to soap—everything, that is, except the food we eat every day.

The inclusion of soybeans in our daily menus is looked upon as an emergency measure, an additive that we'll keep for future use when things get really tight. Actually this is a rather shortsighted viewpoint, because soybeans contain up to 40% protein and are full of vitamin B, all of which stretches the nutritional value of anything they touch.

The green edible bush soybean is the best and fastest sprouter and, when steamed or roasted before using imparts an intriguing, nutlike flavor. Roasted and ground sprouts could be a reasonable substitute for peanut butter in cupcakes, muffins or cookies. Breakfast would be a whole new world with soybean sprout cupcakes or cookies, fruit and milk. A soy sprout-mushroom soufflé is a beautifully healthy way of eating lunch or dinner. A little meat goes a long way, nutritionally, when it is enhanced with soybean stuffing. Do not underestimate the power of this little bean and the new flavors it will give to your everyday meals.

Note: To steam soybeans and all other bean sprouts put them in a sieve or colander over a pan of water. Cover and steam over medium heat for 10–15 minutes. Bigger beans may take longer. Give them the taste test for tenderness. Put on paper towels to drain.

To roast any bean: spread on baking sheet and put in 300° oven for 15 minutes until skins are wrinkled. This is really drying out. Again the taste test. They will have a definitely nutty flavor. To grind: always steam or roast *before* grinding. Then put through the finest blade of a meat grinder. A blender does not work satisfactorily for beans unless incorporating with liquids. This process does not apply to grains. Generally, for use in breads, grains are ground without roasting or steaming.

METHOD: jar, plastic container or screen
TIME: 3–4 days
LENGTH: ½"–1½"
YIELD: 1 cup makes 3 cups

A word of caution: Soybean sprouts will ferment rapidly in hot weather and are more satisfactory to work with beyond the heat of summer.

CURRIED CREAM CHEESE ROLL

1 8 oz. pkg. cream cheese
¼ cup chutney, chopped fine
2 tsp. curry powder
1 cup roasted and ground soy sprouts

Soften cream cheese.
Mix with chopped chutney, and curry powder to taste.
Chill.
Form into a roll.
Roll in soy sprouts, completely covering outside.
Chill and serve with crackers.

Any leftover makes a good stuffing for celery or tomatoes or spread on bread for a chicken sandwich.

CHICKEN LIVER PÂTÉ

1 lb. chicken livers
½ cup melted butter
¼ cup heavy cream
3 tbsp. brandy
½ small onion, chopped
½ garlic clove, chopped
¼ tsp. allspice
1 tsp. dry mustard
½ cup steamed soy sprouts
1 tsp. salt
  freshly-ground pepper

Put livers in saucepan and cover with water. Add salt.
Bring to boil; reduce heat and simmer, covered, until tender, about 10 minutes. Drain.
Put livers in blender with all ingredients. Blend until smooth.
Pack into crock and refrigerate, covered, for 24 hours.

Use as a spread on toast or as stuffing for raw mushrooms or celery.

A BASIC VEGETABLE SOUP

SERVES 6–8

2 tbsp. butter or margarine
1 tbsp. oil
1 green pepper, chopped
2 medium onions, chopped
1 clove garlic, minced (optional)
1 leek, white part only chopped (optional)
3 large carrots, peeled and diced
3 medium potatoes, peeled and diced
4 tomatoes, peeled and chopped
8 cups liquid, all beef bouillon or half bouillon and half water
  salt to taste
  freshly-ground pepper
1 cup lima beans, fresh or frozen
1 cup peas, fresh or frozen
1 cup green beans in 1-inch lengths
1 cup zucchini, diced
½ cup barley
2 tbsp. chopped parsley
½ tsp. thyme
1 tsp. basil
2 cups soy bean sprouts
  grated Parmesan cheese

In large soup kettle, heat oil and butter. Sauté green pepper, onion, garlic, leek and carrots until soft. Add potatoes, tomatoes, liquid, salt and pepper. Bring to boil. Reduce heat to simmer and cook, covered, for 1 hour.

Add remaining ingredients except soy sprouts and cheese. Continue simmering for 1 hour.

At this point the soup may be frozen for future use.

Fifteen minutes before serving, add soy sprouts and heat through.

Serve hot, sprinkled with grated Parmesan cheese and parsley.

This is a complete meal with the addition of bread, salad and cheese.

BAKED BASS WITH STUFFING

SERVES 6

1 5 lb. striped bass, cleaned with head and tail left on
1 cup fine bread crumbs
½ red sweet pepper, chopped fine
2 stalks celery, chopped fine
½ medium onion, minced
½ cup steamed soy sprouts, chopped fine (do not grind)
2 tbsp. chopped chives
1 tbsp. chopped parsley
   salt and pepper to taste
   juice of ½ lemon
2 tbsp. butter
2 tbsp. snipped fresh dill
4 tbsp. melted butter

Preheat oven to 400°.
Combine and mix together the crumbs, red pepper, celery, onion, sprouts, chives, parsley, salt and pepper.
Stuff the fish with this mixture and skewer or sew up opening.
Place fish on foil on a large baking sheet.
Sprinkle with lemon juice and dot with butter, salt and pepper.
Bake for 45 minutes.
Remove to serving platter and pour over the melted butter mixed with fresh dill.

MEAT BALLS IN RED WINE

SERVES 6

1½ lbs. ground chuck
1 cup steamed soy sprouts, ground
1 clove garlic, minced
3 tbsp. grated onion
2 tsp. dry mustard
salt to taste
freshly-ground pepper
1 egg
½ tsp. thyme
1 tsp. oregano
1 tsp. soy sauce
flour for dredging
2 tbsp. bacon fat or oil
1 cup strong coffee
½ cup dry red wine
½ cup beef bouillon
1 cup sour cream
2 tbsp. flour

Put first 11 ingredients in bowl and mix together, blending well.
Form into walnut sized balls.
Roll in flour.
Heat bacon fat in heavy pan to smoking.
Quickly sauté meatballs in fat until brown on all sides.
Turn heat to low.
Add coffee, wine and bouillon.
Cover and simmer for 30 minutes.
Mix flour with sour cream.
Stir into liquid in pan.
Cook uncovered for 5 minutes. Serve hot with rice.

STUFFED FLANK STEAK

SERVES 6

1 2½ lb. flank steak
1 cup steamed soy sprouts
3 hardboiled eggs, quartered
10 carrot strips
3 tbsp. chopped parsley
2 cloves garlic, minced
2 tbsp. grated Parmesan cheese
   salt to taste
   freshly-ground pepper
1 tbsp. each butter and oil
1 cup red wine
1½ cups beef bouillon
2 tsp. potato flour or cornstarch
2 tbsp. orange liqueur
   chopped parsley for garnish
8 orange slices or quarters

With sharp knife, cut through steak horizontally to within ½ inch of back edge. Steak will open up, still attached on one side, and be double in size. Pound between pieces of wax paper until uniformly thin.

Arrange egg quarters and carrot slices alternately on meat. Run them the long way because you are going to roll the meat starting at the longest side.

Sprinkle the soy sprouts, parsley, garlic, cheese and seasonings over the meat.

Roll up and cut if necessary to fit pan. Tie firmly with string.

Heat oil and butter in large skillet and brown meat on all sides.

Add wine and simmer until reduced by about half.

Add beef bouillon. Cover and simmer over low heat until meat is tender— about 1½ hours.

Remove meat from pan to serving platter and slice in ½-inch slices.

Dissolve potato flour in orange liqueur.

Stir into liquid in pan and cook over medium heat until thickened.

Pour sauce over meat.

Garnish platter with chopped parsley and orange slices.

SHRIMP AND CUCUMBERS

SERVES 2 – 3

2 tbsp. butter
2 tbsp. oil
2 large cucumbers, peeled, seeded and cut into 1-inch pieces
½ lb. raw shrimp, peeled and cut in halves
1 cup soy bean sprouts, steamed for 10 minutes
   salt to taste
   freshly-ground pepper
1 tbsp. snipped fresh dill or 1 tsp. dried dill
1 tsp. sugar

In large skillet, heat butter and oil.
Sauté cucumbers for 2 minutes. Remove.
Add shrimp to pan and sauté for 5 minutes until pink and firm.
Add soy sprouts and stir and sauté for 5 minutes.
Put cucumbers back in pan and season with salt, pepper and sugar.
Sprinkle dill over top.
Serve when heated through.

TOMATOES AND BEANS AU GRATIN

SERVES 4

2 slices bacon, chopped
1½ cup onion, chopped
3 medium tomatoes, peeled and chopped
salt to taste
freshly-ground pepper
2 cups soy bean sprouts, steamed for 15 minutes
½ cup heavy cream
1 cup grated Parmesan cheese

Preheat oven to 375°.
In large skillet, fry bacon until just crisp.
Add onion and cook until wilted over medium heat.
Stir in tomatoes and bring to a boil.
Reduce heat and simmer for 15 minutes, uncovered.
Season.
Place steamed soy sprouts in flat baking dish.
Bring cream to a boil and add to tomato sauce.
Pour sauce over bean sprouts.
Sprinkle with cheese.
Bake until heated through and top is lightly browned.

NOTE: Any leftover will make a good filling for an omelet.

BAKED EGGPLANT AND TOMATOES

SERVES 6 – 8

2 medium eggplants, unpeeled
6 large tomatoes, peeled and sliced
2 tbsp. butter or margarine
 salt to taste
 freshly-ground pepper
1½ green peppers, seeded and cut into strips
1 large onion, peeled and cut up
4 slices bacon
½ cup steamed soy sprouts

Preheat oven to 350°.
Butter a 3-qt. flat baking dish.
Cut eggplants into ½-inch slices.
Put half of eggplant slices on bottom of baking dish.
Cover with half of tomato slices.
Dot with butter, salt and pepper.
Cover with remaining eggplant and tomato slices.
Through fine blade of meat grinder put green pepper, onion, bacon and
 soy sprouts.
Spread this ground mixture evenly over top of tomatoes.
Bake for 30 minutes until eggplant is tender.
Remove excess liquid from bottom of baking dish.

MUSHROOM SOUFFLÉ

SERVES 6

3 tbsp. butter
1 tbsp. chopped shallots
½ lb. finely-chopped mushrooms
½ cup steamed soy sprouts, finely chopped
3 tbsp. flour
1 cup milk
    salt to taste
    freshly-ground pepper
½ tsp. ground nutmeg
4 egg yolks
5 egg whites

Preheat oven to 375°.
In large skillet, melt butter. Add shallots, mushrooms and soy sprouts.
Simmer over low heat for 15 minutes.
Sprinkle flour over mushroom mixture and cook 5 minutes.
Add milk and cook, stirring, until mixture thickens.
Season with salt, pepper and nutmeg.
Remove from heat and stir in yolks, one at a time.
Beat whites until stiff but not dry and fold into mixture.
Pour into a greased 1½-qt. soufflé dish.
Bake for 25–30 minutes until just firm.

SPINACH TIMBALES

SERVES 6

1 tbsp. butter or margarine
1 tbsp. flour
½ cup chicken bouillon
½ cup milk
  salt to taste
  freshly-ground pepper
2 cups cooked spinach, well drained
3 eggs
½ cup grated cheddar or Swiss cheese
½ cup steamed and ground soy sprouts
½ tsp. ground nutmeg

Preheat oven to 325°.

In saucepan melt butter with flour. Cook, stirring over medium heat for 2 minutes. Add bouillon and milk. Cook, stirring, until thick and smooth. Cool slightly.

Put spinach in bowl. Add eggs, cheese, sprouts and seasonings. Mix all together.

Add cream sauce and blend all together.

Place in well greased custard cups and place cups in pan of hot water.

Bake for 20 minutes until firm.

Let stand 5 minutes.

Unmold onto rounds of toast.

Serve for lunch with a mushroom sauce and broiled tomatoes.

TORTINO OF ARTICHOKES

SERVES 2

4 artichoke hearts, drained and dried on paper towel
1 tbsp. lemon juice
  flour for dredging
1 tbsp. butter
2 tbsp. oil
4 eggs
¼ cup steamed soy sprouts, ground
  salt to taste
  freshly-ground pepper
2 tbsp. milk

Preheat oven to 350°.
Slice artichoke hearts thin, vertically.
Sprinkle with lemon juice.
Roll in flour.
Heat butter and oil in heavy ovenproof skillet.
Cook artichokes slowly in butter until golden, turning frequently.
Beat eggs, soy sprouts, salt, pepper and milk together with fork.
Pour over artichokes and place in oven.
Cook for 5–10 minutes until eggs are set but not dry.

SIAMESE FRIED RICE

SERVES 4-6

2 tbsp. bacon fat or peanut oil
2 cups chopped onion
2 cups cooked rice
2 eggs beaten with 2 tbsp. soy sauce or more to taste
1 cup cooked chicken, diced
1 cup steamed soy sprouts
  salt to taste
  freshly-ground pepper

In large skillet or wok, heat fat.
Add onion and sauté, stirring, until golden.
Stir in rice and sauté for 3 minutes.
Add egg mixture, turning it into rice. Do not keep stirring or rice will become sticky.
Add chicken and soy sprouts, turning carefully once or twice.
Serve when heated through.

Some kind of spicy relish such as chutney goes well with this, plus cucumbers in yogurt and a fruit dessert.

SAVORY POTATOES

SERVES 6

6 potatoes, cooked, peeled and cubed
2 tbsp. butter
½ cup diced celery
⅓ cup minced onion
¼ cup diced green pepper
1 cup steamed soy sprouts
⅓ cup vinegar
  salt to taste
  freshly-ground pepper
1 tsp. Dijon mustard
⅓ cup melted butter

Preheat broiler.
Put potatoes in large bowl.
In skillet heat butter. Sauté celery, onion and green pepper until wilted,
      about 5 minutes.
Add vegetables and soy sprouts to cubed potatoes.
Mix together vinegar, mustard, salt and pepper.
Pour over potatoes and toss gently to mix.
Spoon into shallow baking dish.
Pour melted butter over all.
Broil 4 to 5 inches from heat until heated through and golden.

SWEET POTATO CROQUETTES

8 TWO-INCH CROQUETTES

1 lb. sweet potatoes or yams
2 tbsp. butter
2 tbsp. cream
1 tbsp. brandy or orange juice
   salt to taste
   freshly-ground pepper
   flour
½ cup soy sprouts, roasted and ground
   butter for sautéeing

Cook potatoes whole in boiling water until soft.
Peel while warm and place in bowl.
Heat together the butter and cream until butter is melted.
Mash potatoes with butter and cream, brandy, salt and pepper.
Make into small cakes and dredge in flour, then coat with soy sprouts.
Refrigerate.
Sauté in butter until crusty and golden.

NOTE: You may add ½ tsp. of ginger, nutmeg or cinnamon if you wish. Serve with ham or pork and apples.

CORN FRITTERS

SERVES 4

1 cup corn kernels, fresh, frozen or canned
1 egg
¼ cup flour
½ tsp. baking powder
1 tsp. sugar
¼ cup steamed soy sprouts, chopped
   salt to taste
   freshly-ground pepper
2 tbsp. bacon fat or butter

Put all ingredients except fat into bowl and mix well.
Heat fat in heavy skillet.
Drop corn mixture by spoonfuls into fat and cook over medium-high heat.
   Turn when browned on one side.
Serve immediately.

These are a good accompaniment for ham or chicken or as a breakfast dish
   with or without bacon strips.

HOT BACON ROLLS

SERVES 4–5

8 slices bacon, cut in halves
4 tbsp. soft peanut butter
6 tbsp. steamed soy sprouts, ground

Preheat oven to 425°.
Blend together with fork the peanut butter and soy sprouts.
Spread on bacon slices.
Roll up and secure with plain round toothpick (not plastic).
Bake for 12 minutes, turning once so bacon will cook on both sides.

NOTE: These may be made ahead and refrigerated or frozen uncooked.

OATMEAL COOKIE MIX

**2 CUPS MIX MAKES
12 COOKIES**

3 cups unbleached white flour
2½ cups sugar
1 tsp. baking powder
2 tsp. salt
1 cup butter or margarine
3 cups regular rolled oats
1 cup soy sprouts, roasted and ground

Put flour, sugar, baking powder and salt all together in large bowl. Cut in
    shortening until mixture resembles coarse meal.
Add oats and soy sprouts and mix well.

This basic mix can be kept in the refrigerator for 2–3 weeks.
Use as follows:
Preheat oven to 375°.

2 cups mix
1 egg
1 tbsp. milk
1 tsp. vanilla or 1 tsp. cinnamon and ¼ tsp. nutmeg
½ cup chopped nuts or raisins or chocolate chips or coconut

Put all ingredients in bowl and mix together, blending well.
Drop by tsp. on greased baking sheet.
Bake for 12–15 minutes.
Remove to racks to cool.

CARROT CAKE

½ cup butter or margarine
½ cup white sugar
½ cup brown sugar
2 eggs, separated
  grated rind of 1 orange
½ cup roasted soy sprouts, chopped fine
¾ cup finely grated carrot
1 tsp. cinnamon
½ tsp. ground nutmeg
2 tsp. baking powder
1½ cups flour
½ tsp. salt
½ cup milk

Preheat oven to 350°.
With mixer beat together butter and sugars until light.
Beat in egg yolks, one at a time.
Beat in orange rind, soy sprouts and carrots.
Mix together spices, baking powder, salt and flour.
Add alternately with milk, mixing well.
Beat whites until stiff but not dry.
Fold into batter.
Pour batter into greased 9-inch square pan or 8 x 5-inch loaf pan.
Bake for 40–45 minutes until cake tests done.
Frost with orange glaze or caramel icing.

BUTTERMILK SPICE CAKE

4 tbsp. butter or margarine
1 cup light brown sugar
1 egg
1½ cups unbleached white flour
½ tsp. soda
1 tsp. baking powder
½ tsp. salt
½ cup buttermilk
¼ tsp. mace
1 tsp. cinnamon

Topping:
½ cup flour
¼ cup butter or margarine
½ cup light brown sugar
½ cup roasted and ground soy sprouts

Preheat oven to 350°.
Make topping by putting all ingredients in bowl and working together with
    fingers, blending well. Set aside.
In mixing bowl, cream together butter and sugar until light.
Beat in egg.
Mix together all dry ingredients.
Add to butter mixture alternately with buttermilk.
Blend well.
Pour into buttered 9-inch square pan.
Cover with topping.
Bake for 35–40 minutes until cake tests done.

This is good for breakfast with sautéed bananas or tomatoes.

BLENDER CUSTARD

SERVES 6

3 eggs
2 cups milk
½ cup sugar
½ tsp. salt
½ cup roasted and ground soy sprouts
1 tsp. vanilla
  ground nutmeg

Preheat oven to 350°.
Put all ingredients except nutmeg in blender.
Blend on high speed for 20 seconds.
Pour into 6 custard cups.
Sprinkle nutmeg over tops.
Place cups in pan of hot water.
Bake for 30–40 minutes until set.

This makes a good after-school snack, and the flavor may be varied to suit the individual taste.

HONEY BALLS

A B O U T 1 D O Z E N

½ cup honey
1 cup pitted dates, chopped
1 cup roasted and ground soy sprouts
½ tsp. vanilla
  pinch of salt
1 cup fresh coconut

Mix all ingredients except coconut together in bowl.
Roll into small balls and dip into coconut, covering all sides.
Refrigerate.

NOTE: The easiest way to cut up dates is with floured scissors. Fresh coconut is less expensive and more flavorful than the packaged. To prepare: With icepick or knitting needle, poke holes in the three "eyes" of the coconut. Let drain until *all* milk is out. Preheat oven to 350°. Put coconut in oven for 15 minutes. If it doesn't crack open by itself, hit it with a hammer. Pry the outer shell away from the meat. With a knife, cut off the dark inner skin. Grate the white meat on a grater or in the blender. Pack into small plastic bags and freeze. One orange-sized coconut will yield 2 cups meat.

GARBANZO BEANS

A "new" food item to be found on the grocery shelves these days among the cans of specialities labeled "International" is the garbanzo or chick pea, also called *ceci* in Italy. Columbus would certainly be surprised to know that the little pebble-like nuggets that he transported to the New World for basic sustenance are now touted as gourmet food. Like the soybean, the garbanzo is high in protein and its A and C content increases when sprouted. Also like the soybean, it should be steamed before using in uncooked dishes. After sprouting the beans, dry them on paper towels; then refrigerate in plastic containers up to four days.

The garbanzo has an outer skin that you may wish to slip off after roasting, just for appearances sake. The flavor? Fresh, crunchy and nutty—a perfect complement to an onion, tomato and corn casserole and an intriguing addition to individual beef pot pies. Roasted and ground, garbanzos can be whipped into a blender ice cream dessert or combined with wheat germ and cheese to crisply-coat a boned chicken breast. Deep fried garbanzos can be part of the condiment tray for a lamb curry dinner.

Poor Columbus, he didn't know what he was missing.

METHOD: jar, plastic container or screen
TIME: 2–3 days
LENGTH: ½-inch
YIELD: ½ cup makes 1½ cups

PARMESAN CHICKEN BREASTS

2 whole chicken breasts, about 1 lb. each
½ cup buttermilk
½ cup roasted and ground garbanzo sprouts
½ cup toasted wheat germ
½ cup grated Parmesan cheese
  salt to taste
  freshly-ground pepper
4–6 tbsp. butter or margarine
4 lemon slices
2 tbsp. chopped parsley

Cut breasts in half. Skin and bone each half.

Put buttermilk in shallow dish.

Combine sprouts, wheat germ, cheese and seasonings in another shallow dish.

Dip raw chicken breasts first in buttermilk, then in sprout mixture, covering completely.

Refrigerate for 1 hour.

Heat butter in large skillet.

Sauté breasts, turning frequently, until done through and brown on all sides.

Garnish with lemon slices and chopped parsley.

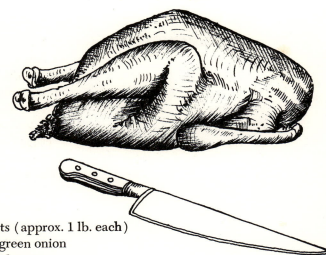

CHICKEN SUPREME

SERVES 4

2 large whole chicken breasts (approx. 1 lb. each)
2 tbsp. chopped shallots or green onion
¼ cup shredded Mozzarella cheese
¼ cup roasted and ground garbanzo sprouts
   salt to taste
   freshly-ground pepper
   juice of ½ a lemon
1 tbsp. butter or margarine

Preheat oven to 425°.
Skin and bone chicken breasts.
Cut each one in half.
Between wax paper, pound breasts until they are thinner and flatter.
Put ½ tbsp. shallots and 1 tbsp. each cheese and sprouts in the center of each breast half.
Roll up, tucking in the sides.
Place in a buttered shallow pan.
Sprinkle over the lemon juice, salt, pepper and dot with butter.
Cover tightly with foil.
Bake for 20 minutes.
Serve with a Bechamel sauce and additional ground sprouts sprinkled over the sauce.

TURKISH MEATBALLS

SERVES 4

1 lb. lean ground lamb
1 egg
¼ cup dry bread crumbs
½ tsp. cinnamon
¼ tsp. mint (optional)
  salt to taste
  freshly-ground pepper
2 tbsp. oil
½ cup chopped onion
1 apple, peeled and diced
1 cup chicken stock
2 tbsp. ginger marmalade
2 tsp. curry powder or to taste
1 cup garbanzo sprouts
1 tsp. potato flour or cornstarch dissolved in 1 tbsp. cold water

Put lamb, egg, crumbs, cinnamon, mint and salt and pepper in bowl. Blend together and shape into marble sized balls.
Heat oil in large skillet and brown lamb balls on all sides.
Remove from pan.
Add onion and sauté until soft.
Add apple, chicken stock, marmalade and curry powder to pan.
Blend together and taste for seasoning.
Put meatballs and sprouts in sauce.
Cover pan and simmer over low heat for 30 minutes.
Stir in potato flour dissolved in water and cook until sauce is thick and smooth.

Serve with fried bananas, chutney and rice.

NOTE: Curry powders vary greatly in intensity of flavor, so taste as you go.

ARMENIAN LAMB AND EGGPLANT

SERVES 6

1 large eggplant, peeled and cubed
½ cup celery, chopped
1 medium onion, chopped
3 tbsp. oil
1½ lbs. lean ground lamb
1 cup garbanzo sprouts, chopped
  salt to taste
  freshly-ground pepper
1 tsp. fresh snipped dill
½ lb. pasta shells, cooked and drained
2 cups tomato sauce
¼ cup grated Parmesan cheese
½ cup cubed Mozzarella cheese

Preheat oven to 350°.
In large skillet heat oil.
Sauté eggplant quickly and remove to bowl.
Sauté celery and onion until soft. Remove to bowl with eggplant.
Toss together and season with salt and pepper.
In skillet sauté lamb until it loses pinkness. Add garbanzo sprouts and sauté for 3 minutes.
Season lamb mixture with salt, pepper and dill.
In 3 qt. casserole dish, place eggplant mixture on bottom.
Pour over 1 cup tomato sauce and sprinkle with Parmesan cheese.
Put in pasta shells.
Cover pasta with lamb mixture.
Pour on remaining tomato sauce and sprinkle cubed Mozzarella cheese over top.
Bake for 30 minutes.

BAKED LAMB SHANKS

SERVES 4

4 large lamb shanks well trimmed of fat
1 cup garbanzo sprouts
2 cloves garlic, minced
2 medium onions, chopped
  juice of 1 lemon
3 tbsp. chopped parsley
1 tsp. chopped mint
  salt to taste
  freshly-ground pepper
½ tsp. cinnamon
2 tomatoes, peeled and sliced (fresh or canned)
1 cup dry Vermouth

Preheat oven to 400°.
Place lamb shanks in 2 qt. baking dish.
Sprinkle sprouts over shanks.
Pour over all ingredients.
Cover tightly.
Roast for 2 hours.
Remove lamb shanks and reduce sauce by boiling hard until it thickens.
    Taste for seasoning and pour over lamb shanks.
Sprinkle with additional parsley.

Serve with rice or kasha, green beans and honey cake.

INDIVIDUAL PORK PIES

SERVES 6

3 lbs. lean pork cut in 1-inch cubes
flour for dredging
salt to taste
freshly-ground pepper
pork or bacon fat
2 medium onions, coarsely chopped
2 cloves garlic, chopped
white wine
1 tsp. sage
1 tbsp. chopped parsley
1 cup garbanzo bean sprouts
1 recipe basic pie pastry

Mix together the salt, pepper and flour.
Dredge pork cubes in mixture.
In large skillet heat fat and brown meat on all sides.
Remove meat and add onions and garlic.
Sauté for 5 minutes.
Return to pan and pour over enough wine to cover meat.
Cover pan and reduce heat to simmer.
Cook for 1½ hours.
Remove cover and check for liquid. If dry, add more wine.
Add garbanzo sprouts, sage and parsley.
Cover and cook for ½ hour longer until meat and sprouts are tender.
Cool and refrigerate overnight.
Skim off fat.
Divide into six individual baking dishes.
Cover the top of each with ½-inch thick piece of pastry.
Preheat oven to 400°.
Bake for 45 minutes until crust is browned.

Serve with sautéed apple rings and broccoli.

CORN AND TOMATO BAKE

SERVES 6

1 pkg. frozen corn or 1½ cups fresh corn kernels
1 tsp. sugar
  salt to taste
  freshly-ground pepper
1 cup garbanzo bean sprouts
1 medium onion, thinly sliced
2 large tomatoes, peeled and chopped or 1½ cups canned tomatoes, drained
½ cup buttered seasoned bread crumbs

Preheat oven to 350°.
Butter a 1½-qt. baking dish.
Spread corn in bottom.
Sprinkle over the sugar, salt and pepper.
Put sprouts on top of corn.
Arrange onion slices over sprouts.
Put tomatoes on top of sprouts and season again.
Cover with buttered crumbs.
Bake uncovered for 30 minutes.

FRUIT STUFFING

½ cup chopped prunes
¼ cup Madeira wine
½ cup garbanzo sprouts, chopped
1 medium tart apple
1 cup bread crumbs
1 small onion, chopped
2 stalks celery, chopped
2 tbsp. butter or margarine
  salt to taste
  freshly-ground pepper
½ tsp. ground nutmeg

Soak prunes in Madeira for 30 minutes.
Heat butter in skillet and sauté onion and celery until soft.
Combine all ingredients including prunes and wine in bowl.
Toss together.

This is enough stuffing for 6 pork chops, one 4 lb. veal breast or 3 Cornish
  game hens.

BAKED ACORN SQUASH

SERVES 4

2 acorn squashes
4 tbsp. butter or margarine
4 tbsp. brown sugar
2 tsp. ground ginger
12 small white onions, cooked
4 tbsp. whole garbanzo sprouts
   salt to taste
   freshly-ground pepper

Preheat oven to 400°.
Split squashes and remove seeds and strings from centers.
Place in baking pan and cover tightly.
Bake for 30 minutes.
Remove from oven. Uncover and fill centers with butter, sugar, ginger, onions and sprouts.
Season to taste.
Return to oven and bake, uncovered, for 30 minutes longer.

SPINACH SALAD

SERVES 6

2 lbs. fresh spinach leaves
½ lb. fresh mushrooms
1 medium red onion
1 cup garbanzo sprouts, steamed and dried on paper towel
1 hardboiled egg yolk
   vinaigrette dressing

Stem spinach leaves and wash and dry well.
Leave in towels in refrigerator until ready to use.
Slice mushrooms.
Slice red onion thinly.
Into large salad bowl put spinach leaves, mushrooms, onion, and garbanzo
   sprouts.
Toss together.
Add a small amount of dressing and toss.
Dressing should coat leaves but not remain in bottom of bowl.
Sieve egg yolk over top and serve.

WINY FRUIT RELISH

1 15-oz. box mixed dried fruit
1 cup sugar
1½ cups dry white wine
½ cup brandy
1 cinnamon stick
2 lemon slices
½ cup garbanzo sprouts

In 2-qt. glass container, place dried fruit.
In saucepan put remaining ingredients.
Bring to a boil, stirring until sugar dissolves.
Pour over fruit and mix well.
Cover and let stand for 3 days before using.

Use as a relish with pork, ham or game.
Serve as a dessert with custard sauce or whipped cream.
Purée fruit in blender and use as a soufflé base.

BANANA BREAD

½ cup butter or margarine
¾ cup light brown sugar
3 medium bananas, mashed
2 eggs
1½ cups flour
1 tsp. salt
1½ tsp. baking powder
¼ cup roasted and ground garbanzo sprouts
¼ cup roasted sunflower sprouts
   juice of half a lemon

Preheat oven to 350°.
Cream butter and sugar until light and smooth.
Add lemon juice to bananas.
Beat in eggs, one at a time.
Mix flour, salt and baking powder together.
Add dry ingredients to butter mixture alternately with mashed bananas.
Stir in sprouts.
Pour batter into greased large or two small loaf pans.
Bake for 40–50 minutes until bread tests done.
Turn out onto racks.
Slice when completely cooled.

ORANGE MUFFINS

MAKES 12

1 cup flour
¼ cup sugar
½ tsp. salt
3 tsp. baking powder
2 eggs
½ cup orange juice
2 tbsp. melted butter or margarine
½ cup roasted garbanzo sprouts, chopped
   grated rind of half an orange

Preheat oven to 425°.
Put all dry ingredients in large bowl.
Add eggs, orange juice and butter all at once.
Beat together quickly with spoon.
Mix in sprouts and orange rind.
Fill buttered muffin tins ¾ full.
Bake for 15–20 minutes.

WINY FRUIT RELISH CAKE

3 eggs, separated
⅔ cup sugar
⅓ cup of fruit wine
¾ cup regular white flour
¾ cup roasted and ground garbanzo sprouts
¼ lb. butter melted and cooled slightly
½ cup fruit from relish, chopped fine*
  pinch of salt

Preheat oven to 350°.
In large bowl beat yolks, adding sugar gradually.
Add wine and blend in.
Add flour and mix well.
Stir in ground sprouts.
Stir in butter, mixing well.
Add chopped fruit.
Beat whites until stiff but not dry, with a pinch of salt.
Fold whites into batter.
Pour into one 8-inch greased layer cake tin or two 5 x 2½-inch loaf tins.
Bake for 35–40 minutes until cake tests done.
Let stand 10 minutes.
Turn out onto racks.
Cool before cutting.
* NOTE: See previous recipe.

RUM SAUCE

MAKES 1 CUP

3 tbsp. butter
½ cup brown sugar
¼ cup water
½ cup coconut
¼ cup roasted garbanzo sprouts, chopped
2 tbsp. dark rum

In saucepan put butter, sugar and water. Cook, stirring, until sugar is dissolved. Add remaining ingredients.
Simmer for 5 minutes.
Serve warm over ice cream or baked bananas.

COFFEE PARFAIT

ABOUT 4 CUPS

1 cup roasted and ground garbanzo sprouts
1 cup heavy cream, whipped
⅛ cup sugar
¼ cup water
3 tbsp. instant coffee
1 tbsp. rum
3 egg yolks

Combine ½ cup sprouts and whipped cream in a bowl.
Put sugar, water and coffee in saucepan and bring to a boil.
Cook, stirring, until sugar is dissolved.
Put egg yolks and rum in blender.
With motor on high speed, pour coffee mixture into blender in a steady stream.
Turn off blender and fold egg mixture into whipped cream.
Spoon parfait into individual glasses or refrigerator tray.
Sprinkle remaining sprouts on top.
Freeze several hours until firm.

ALFALFA

If you know that the Arabs fed alfalfa to their horses to make them strong and swift, it is a little difficult to accept the fact that we too can eat this cattle forage. After all, we're not planning to run races with horses. But if we know the content of alfalfa and are given some suggestions as to how it can be made definitely enjoyable, then it is worth acknowledging as an excellent seed for sprouting.

Alfalfa is 35% protein, at its highest, when the root is an eighth inch long. That is the time to grind the sprouts in the fine blade of a meat grinder and add them to light cottage cheese rolls, a honeyed whole wheat nut bread or a sweet pie crust. When sprouted, this interesting grain also contains vitamins D, E, K and C and the minerals phosphorus, iron and silicon—a lot of nourishment to add to cakes, breads and even cheese.

Spread alfalfa sprouts on a baking sheet and dry them in a 300 degree oven for about 45 minutes and they can be used in many recipes calling for nuts. However, keep in mind that drying decreases the total amount from 1 cup down to ⅛ cup. Let alfalfa sprouts grow to 1-inch length and put them in the sun for a few hours; they will greatly increase their chlorophyll content and add a crunchy, leafy character to your salads. This is what can be done with a little ordinary cattle fodder and a lot of imagination.

METHOD: jar
LENGTH: 1-inch or ⅛-inch depending on use
TIME: 24 hours for ⅛-inch, 3–4 days for 1-inch
YIELD: ¼ cup makes 1½ cups

BAKED CHEESE SANDWICH

SERVES 6

6 slices whole wheat bread
¾ cup white wine
1 cup grated cheddar cheese
1 cup alfalfa sprouts, ⅛-inch
2 eggs
3 tbsp. butter
3 slices bacon, cooked and crumbled

Preheat oven to 350°.
Place bread on greased baking sheet.
Sprinkle wine over bread.
Beat together the cheese, eggs and sprouts.
Spread on bread slices.
Dot with butter.
Bake for 10–15 minutes until puffy.
Garnish with crumbled bacon.

CORNBREAD WITH BACON

4 slices bacon
1 cup alfalfa sprouts, about ¼-inch
1 cup white flour
1 cup stone-ground yellow cornmeal
3 tsp. baking powder
⅓ cup sugar
½ tsp. salt
1 egg
1 cup milk
¼ cup bacon fat

Preheat oven to 400°.
Cook bacon and remove to drain. Reserve ¼ cup bacon fat.
Chop bacon fine with sprouts.
In large mixing bowl put flour, cornmeal, baking powder, sugar and salt.
Add egg, milk and fat all at once.
Stir together quickly.
Add bacon and sprouts and mix well.
Spoon batter into greased 8-inch square pan.
Bake for 20 minutes until done.

OAT BREAD

YIELD: 3 SMALL
LOAVES AND 12 ROLLS
OR 2 LARGE LOAVES

1 cup rolled oats
2 cups water
½ cup molasses
2 tbsp. butter or shortening
1 tsp. salt
2 tbsp. yeast
¼ cup warm water
6–7 cups unbleached white flour
2 cups alfalfa sprouts (⅛-inch)

Bring water to a boil and pour over oats in large bowl.
Add molasses, butter and salt.
Cool to lukewarm.
Add yeast to warm water and let stand until bubbly—about 5 minutes.
Add yeast to oats.
Beat in 3 cups flour and sprouts.
Gradually beat in remaining flour. Mix well.
Turn out onto floured board and knead until dough is smooth, non-sticky and has a slightly "blistered" look. Add more flour if necessary.
Put ball of dough in greased bowl and cover.
Set in warm place to rise until double—about 1½ hours.
Punch down and shape into 3 loaves for 8 x 5-inch pans and 12 rolls.
Cover and let rise again until dough comes almost to tops of pans.
Preheat oven to 375°.
Bake bread for 45 minutes, rolls for 30 minutes.
Turn out and tap with fingers. If bread sounds hollow, it is done.
Cool on racks.

WHOLE WHEAT NUT BREAD

1½ cups whole wheat flour
2 cups unbleached white flour
1 cup ground alfalfa sprouts (⅛-inch)
½ cup honey
1 tsp. salt
1 cup chopped walnuts
2 tsp. baking soda

Preheat oven to 350°.
In large bowl mix together the flours and sprouts.
Stir in soda and salt.
Add honey and blend well.
Fold in walnuts.
Spoon into greased loaf pan.
Bake for 1 hour until bread is firm and has pulled away from the sides of the pan.
Turn out onto rack to cool.

COTTAGE CHEESE ROLLS

YIELD: ABOUT
18 ROLLS

1 tbsp. yeast
¼ cup warm water
1 cup creamed cottage or farmer's cheese
1 egg
½ cup alfalfa sprouts, ⅛-inch long
2 tsp. minced onion
3½ cups white unbleached flour
2 tsp. baking powder
1 tsp. salt
2 tsp. sugar
2 tbsp. softened butter or margarine

Dissolve yeast in warm water for 5 minutes.
In blender put cottage cheese, egg, sprouts and onion. Blend at high speed until smooth.
In large bowl combine flour, baking powder, salt and sugar.
Add yeast, cheese mixture and butter.
Beat together well.
Turn out on floured board and knead until smooth, at least 5 minutes. Add more flour to prevent sticking if necessary.
Place in greased bowl. Cover. Let rise until double.
Punch down. Pinch off pieces and roll into balls, approximately golf ball size. Place in greased baking pans. Cover pans with towel or plastic wrap.
Preheat oven to 375°.
Let rise 20 minutes. Remove pan covering.
Bake for 20–30 minutes until golden.

CRANBERRY MUFFINS

YIELD: ONE DOZEN

¾ cup cranberries, halved
½ cup powdered sugar
2 cups flour
½ cup roasted and ground alfalfa sprouts, ⅛-inch
3 tsp. baking powder
½ tsp. salt
¼ cup sugar
1 egg
1 cup milk
4 tbsp. melted butter or margarine
1 tbsp. grated orange rind

Preheat oven to 350°.
Mix cranberries and sugar in bowl and let stand.
Put dry ingredients together in large bowl.
Add egg, milk and butter all at once.
Mix until dry ingredients are dampened.
Do not beat.
Fold in cranberries and orange rind.
Fill greased muffin tins ⅔ full.
Bake for 20 minutes.

SWEET PIE CRUST

16 graham crackers
¼ cup sugar
¼ cup melted butter or margarine
½ cup alfalfa sprouts (⅛-inch)
½ tsp. cinnamon

Crumble graham crackers into fine crumbs.
Put into bowl with remaining ingredients.
Mix together.
Press into 8-inch pie pan.
Refrigerate for 15 minutes.
Preheat oven to 375°.
Bake pie shell for 8 minutes. Cool.

This is an excellent crust for a butterscotch or pumpkin pie.

CHOCOLATE CRISPS

2 squares unsweetened chocolate
1½ sticks butter or margarine
1 cup sugar
3 tbsp. vanilla
½ cup roasted alfalfa sprouts, ⅛-inch
1 cup regular rolled oats
  grated rind of ½ orange
1 cup white flour

Preheat oven to 350°.
In medium-sized saucepan, melt butter and chocolate over medium heat.
Remove from heat and add sugar, stirring until dissolved.
Beat in remaining ingredients, mixing well.
Drop by tsp. onto greased baking sheet.
Bake for 10 minutes until firm.
Remove to racks.

PRUNE CAKE

½ cup butter
1 cup sugar
2 eggs
1 cup prune pulp
1½ cups white flour
1½ tsp. soda
1 tsp. cinnamon
½ tsp. nutmeg
½ tsp. salt
½ cup roasted alfalfa sprouts, ⅛- to ½-inch
2 tbsp. brandy

Preheat oven to 350°.
In mixing bowl cream together the butter and sugar until smooth.
Beat in eggs one at a time.
Beat in prune pulp.
Mix together the dry ingredients and sprouts.
Add to bowl gradually, blending well.
Stir in brandy.
Turn into greased pans—two 9-inch layer pans or four 5½ x 3-inch loaf pans.
Bake for 40–50 minutes until firm.
Let stand 10 minutes.
Turn out onto racks and cool.

NOTE: To make prune pulp, stew a 12 oz. box of pitted prunes for 5 minutes and put through the food mill.

GRAHAM CAKE ROLL

SERVES 8

1 cup graham cracker crumbs
1 cup roasted alfalfa sprouts, ⅛-inch
1 tsp. baking powder
6 egg yolks
1 cup sugar
1 tsp. vanilla
½ tsp. almond extract
6 egg whites
   pinch of salt
2 cups cream, whipped
1 tbsp. rum
¼ cup confectioner's sugar

Preheat oven to 375°.
Prepare a 15 x 10-inch jelly roll pan; butter pan, line with waxed paper, butter paper.
Combine crumbs, sprouts and baking powder in bowl.
In mixing bowl beat yolks, gradually adding sugar, until light.
Beat in vanilla and almond extracts.
Add crumb mixture and stir in.
Beat whites with pinch of salt until stiff but not dry.
Fold into yolk mixture.
Spread batter in lined pan.
Bake for 15 minutes until cake is firm to the touch.
Turn out onto clean towel. Remove pan.
Let rest for 5 minutes. Strip off paper. Cool.
Beat cream with rum and sugar.
Spread ⅔ of cream over roll.
Roll up.
Spread with remaining cream, covering up cracks if there are any.
Refrigerate until ready to serve.

WHEAT

It seems to be as true today as it has been for many centuries, that the way of our world is determined by our wheat crops. Wheat is still the world's most widely-cultivated food plant and one that would be sorely missed in all kitchens from peasant to palace. It contains little fat and is a good source of protein, vitamin E, niacin and pantothenic acid. It is also so sweet in flavor that a small amount goes a long way when added to other foods such as a pilaf or to light rolls or as the sweet crunchy topping for an apple dessert. Dried hard wheat sprouts can be ground and tucked into almost any cookie or cake batter.

METHOD: jar
TIME: 2–3 days
LENGTH: 1/16-inch
YIELD: 1 cup makes 2½–3 cups

CRÊPES

3 eggs
2 tbsp. melted butter or margarine
1 cup milk
1 tsp. salt
½ cup wheat sprouts
1 cup whole wheat flour
2 tbsp. brandy

Put all ingredients in blender and blend on high speed until smooth.
If you don't have a blender, use whisk or electric mixer.
Strain batter into pitcher.
Refrigerate for 1 hour.
Before using, whisk batter together.
Cook on hot buttered griddle or in crêpe pan.

These can be filled with creamed mushrooms or chicken or a vegetable
mixture such as spinach in a cheese sauce.

KASHA PILAF

SERVES 4

1 cup groats, kasha or wheat pilaf
1 small onion, minced
2 tbsp. butter or margarine
1 egg
2 cups chicken bouillon
  salt to taste
  freshly-ground pepper
2 tbsp. butter
1 cup wheat sprouts
2 tbsp. minced parsley

In large skillet, heat butter. Sauté onion for 2 minutes.
Stir in groats.
Break egg into groats and stir to coat all grains.
Cook, stirring, for 3 minutes.
Add bouillon, salt and a lot of pepper.
Turn heat to medium low and cover pan.
Cook for 20 minutes or until all liquid is absorbed.
Uncover and fluff with fork.
Use fork to stir in 2 tbsp. butter and sprouts.
Heat through and serve immediately with minced parsley for garnish.

ANN SERANNE'S
POPOVER PANCAKE

SERVES 2-3

½ cup flour
¼ cup wheat sprouts
½ cup milk
2 eggs
3 tbsp. butter
½ cup applesauce
2 tbsp. cinnamon-sugar

Preheat oven to 425°.
In blender combine flour, sprouts, milk and eggs. Blend on high speed for
    30 seconds until smooth.
Heat butter in 8-inch skillet with ovenproof handle.
Pour batter into skillet.
Bake for 25 minutes until puffy and golden.
Spread with applesauce and sprinkle with cinnamon-sugar.
Serve immediately.

Excellent for a pre-school breakfast.

CINNAMON RAISIN ROLL

SERVES 6

2 tbsp. yeast
¾ cup warm water
¼ cup buttermilk
4 tbsp. melted butter
2½ cups whole wheat flour
½ cup wheat sprouts
2 tbsp. sugar
2 tsp. baking powder
2 tsp. salt
2 tbsp. cinnamon
1½ cups raisins
½ cup white flour
2 tbsp. softened butter

In large mixing bowl dissolve yeast in warm water.

When it is bubbly, add buttermilk and butter. Stir together.

Mix together the whole wheat flour, sprouts, sugar, baking powder, salt and cinnamon, and beat into yeast mixture.

Beat well for 5 minutes. Stir in raisins.

Turn out onto ½ cup white flour.

Knead well until dough is smooth and shiny and does not stick to board.

Roll into a rectangle 18 x 9 inches. Spread with softened butter.

Cut rectangle in half, making two 9 x 9-inch squares. Roll up.

Place seam side down in buttered pans. Brush with butter.

Cover and let rise until almost double. Dough should be light to the touch.

Preheat oven to 400°.

Bake for 30–35 minutes. Serve warm.

WHOLE WHEAT RISEN ROLLS

YIELD: APPROX.
36 ROLLS

½ cup milk
4 tbsp. butter or margarine
1 tbsp. sugar
1 tsp. salt
1 tbsp. yeast
⅓ cup warm water
2 cups whole wheat flour
¾ cup wheat sprouts, ground
1 egg
1 cup white flour
3 tbsp. melted butter

Scald milk. Pour into large bowl and add butter, sugar and salt.
Cool to lukewarm.
Dissolve yeast in warm water for 5 minutes until bubbly.
Stir into milk with whole wheat flour and sprouts.
Beat together until well mixed.
Cover bowl and let rise in a warm place about 1 hour, until light and spongy.
    (It will not double.)
Punch down and beat in egg and ¾ cup white flour.
Turn out and knead in remaining flour. Dough will be soft but not sticky.
Roll out on floured board to ½-inch thickness.
With round cutter, cut circles of dough.
Brush with melted butter, fold in half, pinching edges together.
Place in 2 buttered pans. Cover and let rise 15 minutes.
Preheat oven to 425°.
Bake for 15 minutes.

BASIC PIE CRUST

YIELD: PASTRY FOR
2-CRUST PIE

1 egg yolk
1 cup wheat sprouts (¼-inch)
4 tbsp. butter or margarine
6 tbsp. vegetable shortening
1 tsp. salt
½ cup whole wheat flour
1½ cups white flour
3–4 tbsp. ice water

Put egg yolk and sprouts in blender and blend on high speed for 20 seconds.
Cream together the butter and shortening in large bowl.
Add flours and salt and mix together with electric mixer or fingers until mixture is like coarse meal.
Mix in egg and sprouts.
Add ice water, 1 tbsp. at a time, mixing dough until it is firm and not sticky.
Wrap in wax paper and refrigerate.

This is a good pie crust for quiches, vegetable tarts or apple pie.

APPLE CRISP

SERVES 6

6 tart apples
juice of 1 lemon
¾ cup white flour
1 cup dark brown sugar
½ cup butter or margarine
½ cup wheat sprouts
1 tsp. ground cinnamon

Preheat oven to 350°.
Butter a shallow 1½-qt. baking dish.
Peel and core apples and cut into 8 sections.
Place apples in dish and sprinkle with lemon juice.
Put remaining ingredients in bowl and mix together with fingers.
Spread over apples.
Bake for 30 minutes.

Serve with ice cream or whipped cream.

WHEAT CRISPS

YIELD: ABOUT 48
COOKIES

½ cup butter or margarine
1 cup brown sugar
1 egg
¼ tsp. baking soda
½ tsp. salt
1 cup flour
1 tsp. vanilla
1 cup chopped wheat sprouts

Preheat oven to 375°.
In bowl cream together the butter and sugar until well blended.
Beat in egg.
Mix together the soda, salt and flour.
Beat in.
Stir in vanilla and sprouts.
Drop by teaspoonfuls onto ungreased cookie sheet.
Bake for 10–12 minutes.

TRITICALE

One exciting thing about this world of ours is that every corner we turn brings a new discovery, invention or idea. The latest in the world of grains is something called Triticale, combining the two botanical terms Triticum for wheat and Secale for rye in a hybrid cross.

Research on this food has been going on for years, and the excitement comes in the fact that Triticale contains much more protein than any of the other cereal grains. It supplies 19 amino acids and more of those usually in short supply, such as lyzene.

When sprouting, Triticale doubles in protein. It is a bit lighter in color than wheat, sprouts faster and is more tender. What it does as a natural additive for breakfast fare, such as waffles, muffins and breads, is obvious. Certainly it's an easy way to introduce added protein into a meal. It should be treated the same way as wheat—ground, blended or dried before incorporating into other ingredients.

METHOD: jar
TIME: 2–3 days
LENGTH: 1/16-inch
YIELD: 1 cup makes 2½ cups

BUTTERMILK PANCAKES

SERVES 3 – 4

1 cup flour
1 tsp. salt
2 tsp. baking powder
2 tsp. sugar
2 eggs
1 cup buttermilk
½ cup Triticale sprouts
3 tbsp. melted butter or margarine

Put all dry ingredients in large bowl.
In blender put eggs, buttermilk and sprouts.
Blend at high speed for 20 seconds until smooth.
Mix liquid quickly with dry ingredients.
Stir in butter.
Cook in skillet as for any pancake.

WAFFLES

SERVES 6–8

1½ cups flour
1 tsp. salt
4 tsp. baking powder
1 tbsp. sugar
2 eggs, separated
2 cups milk
½ cup Triticale sprouts
4 tbsp. melted butter

Combine flour, salt, baking powder and sugar in large bowl.
In blender put egg yolks, milk and sprouts.
Blend for 20 seconds.
Pour blended mixture onto dry ingredients. Combine well.
Add melted butter.
Beat whites stiff but not dry and fold in.
Bake as for any waffle.

NOTE: Triticale sprouts will not completely pulverize in blender but will soften enough to blend in with other ingredients and will not be hard grains when cooked.

Waffles are good not just for breakfast. Try them for Sunday supper with creamed chicken and a salad.

HIGH PROTEIN MUFFINS

YIELD: 1 DOZEN

1 cup whole wheat flour
1 cup white flour
1 tsp. salt
2 tbsp. brown sugar
2 tsp. baking powder
¼ cup Triticale sprouts
1 egg
1 cup milk
4 tbsp. melted butter

Preheat oven to 400°.
Combine in mixing bowl the flours, salt, baking powder and sugar.
In blender put sprouts, egg, milk and butter.
Blend for 20 seconds.
Pour over dry ingredients and mix together with spoon. Stir, do not beat, until well mixed.
Butter a 12-muffin tin. Fill each ⅔ full.
Bake for 20–25 minutes until risen and firm.
Serve hot.

With a fruit and a glass of milk, these muffins make a quick and easy breakfast.

SWEET BREAKFAST BREAD

SERVES 4

½ cup sugar
4 tbsp. butter
1 egg
1 cup flour
¼ cup Triticale sprouts, ground
2½ tsp. baking powder
½ tsp. salt
6 tbsp. milk
½ cup raisins
3 tbsp. sugar mixed with 1 tsp. ground cinnamon

Preheat oven to 350°.
Cream together the sugar and butter until smooth.
Beat in egg.
Mix together the dry ingredients.
Add alternately with milk. Blend well.
Stir in raisins.
Spoon into buttered 8-inch square pan.
Sprinkle cinnamon-sugar over top.
Bake for 25–30 minutes.
Serve warm.

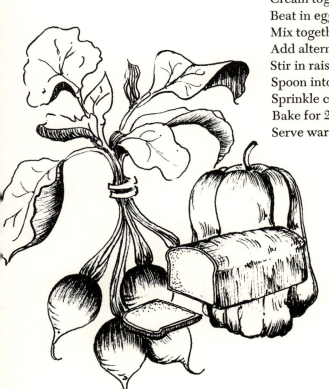

SCOTTISH SCONES

SERVES 4

1½ cups flour
1 tsp. cream of tartar
½ tsp. salt
1 tsp. sugar
1 tsp. baking soda
½ cup Triticale sprouts, ground
¼–½ cup buttermilk

Preheat oven to 425°.
Put all dry ingredients in bowl.
Add enough liquid to make a soft dough.
Turn out on floured board and knead slightly.
Pat into a circle ½-inch thick.
Transfer circle to baking sheet.
Bake for 20 minutes until risen and browned.
Serve immediately with lots of butter and honey.

DATE AND NUT BREAD

YIELD: 3 SMALL LOAVES

1 cup chopped dates
1 cup boiling water
1 cup sugar
1 tbsp. melted butter
1 egg
1½ cups flour
½ cup Triticale sprouts, ground
2 tsp. baking soda
½ tsp. baking powder
½ tsp. salt
1 cup chopped walnuts
½ tsp. vanilla (optional)

Preheat oven to 350°.
Pour boiling water over chopped dates in small bowl. Let stand.
Place sugar in large mixing bowl.
Stir into sugar the butter and egg. Mix well.
Combine all dry ingredients except nuts and mix with sugar.
Stir in dates and water.
Stir in nuts and vanilla. Mix well.
Butter three 5½ x 3-inch loaf pans and spoon batter in, filling ⅔ full.
Bake for 40 minutes until bread tests done.
Run a knife around the edges of the pans and turn out onto racks.
Cool.

BEANS, BEANS, BEANS

The bean—be it lima, red kidney, pinto, great northern, white or fava—is about the richest source of protein in the vegetable kingdom. Beans have been around as a source of food for many a century, and once upon a time they were worshiped. Certain Peruvian Indians believed that beans contained the souls of a special category of the departed, and until the beans sprouted that soul wouldn't go on to the next world.

Beans also have been associated with peasant food, as a source of sustenance for the poor. While kings and princes chewed on their tough roasts and haunches, their underlings delighted in cassoulets, marinated beans and bean ragouts.

Though good sources of iron, niacin, phosphorous and potassium, also vitamins B1 and B2, the one thing against beans (in quantity) is that for many people they are hard to digest and somewhat fattening. This is one good reason for sprouting your dried beans rather than just soaking and using as-is. With sprouting they lose their unpleasant gases and carbohydrates, although they maintain their individual flavors and may be used in any of your favorite bean recipes to good advantage.

All beans mentioned in the following recipes are treated the same way and should be steamed until tender before using, unless otherwise noted. See directions under Soybeans.

METHOD: jar, plastic container or screen
TIME: 4–5 days
LENGTH: ¼–½ inch
YIELD: 1 cup makes 3 cups

BRITTANY COD

SERVES 4

1 lb. salt cod
milk to cover
1½ tbsp. butter
1½ tbsp. flour
1½ cups milk
2 cups sprouted and steamed bush limas or white beans
¼ cup grated Parmesan cheese
½ cup dry bread crumbs
3 tbsp. melted butter

Soak cod overnight in water to cover.
Drain and put in large saucepan. Cover with milk.
Simmer, covered, until fish flakes easily, about 20 minutes.
Do not boil or fish will toughen.
Preheat oven to 350°.
Make sauce by heating butter and flour in saucepan. Cook, stirring for 3 minutes.
Add milk and cook, stirring until thickened slightly.
Layer flaked fish and bean sprouts in shallow greased baking dish.
Pour sauce over all.
Sprinkle cheese and crumbs over top.
Dribble melted butter over crumbs.
Bake for 30 minutes until golden with crust.

VEAL RAGOUT

SERVES 4 – 5

2 lbs. stewing veal, cut in 1-inch cubes
2 tbsp. butter
1 tbsp. oil
  salt to taste
  freshly-ground pepper
3 cups chicken bouillon
½ cup dry white wine
2 3-inch strips orange peel
1 clove garlic, minced
1½ cups canned tomatoes, drained
1 bay leaf
3 sprigs parsley
2 cups sprouted bush limas, not steamed
2 tbsp. butter blended with 2 tbsp. flour

In iron Dutch oven or heavy casserole, heat butter and oil.
Brown meat quickly, turning frequently.
Season.
Add bouillon and wine and cover.
Turn heat to simmer and cook for 1 hour.
Add orange peel, garlic, tomatoes, herbs and bean sprouts.
Cover and cook for 1 hour longer, until meat and vegetables are tender.
Thicken with butter-flour mixture stirred into hot sauce.
Taste and correct seasoning.

Serve with noodles and a salad.

BAKED LAMB AND RICE

SERVES 4–5

3 tbsp. butter
1 tbsp. oil
2 onions, minced
½ cup raw rice
2 cups cooked lamb, cubed
1 cup sprouted limas
4 tomatoes peeled and chopped or 2 cups canned tomatoes, drained
2 cups chicken bouillon
  salt to taste
1 tsp. basil
½ tsp. oregano
1 tbsp. Worcestershire sauce
3 tbsp. minced parsley

Preheat oven to 350°.
In large skillet or saucepan heat oil and butter.
Sauté onion for 3 minutes. Stir in rice and sauté for 2 minutes.
Add lamb, bean sprouts, tomatoes, bouillon, salt and herbs.
Simmer uncovered for 15 minutes.
Transfer to 2-qt. casserole.
Bake for 45 minutes until bubbling and rice is tender.
Sprinkle with minced parsley.

BEEF AND BEANS

SERVES 6

2½ lbs. lean stewing beef, cut in 1-inch cubes
2 large onions, chopped
  salt to taste
  freshly-ground pepper
1 lb. smoked sausage, cut in 1-inch pieces
2 cups sprouted kidney beans, not steamed
1 cup dry red wine
2 cups beef bouillon
1 clove garlic, minced
½ tsp. thyme
1 bay leaf
  grated rind of ½ lemon
2 tbsp. brandy
3 tbsp. chopped parsley

Preheat oven to 325°.
In large 3-qt. casserole put beef, onions, salt and pepper.
Cover and place in oven.
Cook for 1 hour.
Add remaining ingredients except brandy and parsley.
Cover and cook for 1½–2 hours until meat and sprouts are tender. Just before serving stir in brandy and sprinkle parsley over top.

Serve with rice, braised carrots and a salad.

BEANS AND SAUSAGES
IN BEER

SERVES 4 – 6

½ lb. lean pork, cut in ½-inch cubes
1 cup sliced onions
2 tbsp. butter
1 tbsp. oil
1 lb. Kielbasy sausage, skinned and cut in ½-inch rings
12 oz. beer
½ tsp. sage
salt to taste
freshly-ground pepper
1½ cups sprouted pinto beans, steamed 20 minutes
½ cup grated mild cheese

Heat butter and oil in large skillet or Dutch oven.
Brown pork quickly.
Add onions and sauté over medium heat until soft.
Add sausage and beer.
Season.
Cover and simmer for 30 minutes.
Preheat oven to 325°.
In 2-qt. casserole, layer bean sprouts with cooked sausage, onions and pork.
Reduce liquid in Dutch oven slightly by boiling hard.
Pour over contents of casserole.
Sprinkle grated cheese over top.
Bake for 30 minutes, uncovered.

Serve with dark bread, cheese and fruit.

LIMAS WITH BACON DRESSING

SERVES 4

3 cups sprouted limas, steamed until tender
4 slices bacon in 1-inch pieces
2 tbsp. minced onion
⅓ cup tomato juice
1 tsp. vinegar
  salt to taste
  freshly-ground pepper

In heavy saucepan sauté bacon until crisp. Remove bacon pieces to drain.
In 2 tbsp. remaining fat sauté onion briefly.
Stir in tomato juice, vinegar and seasonings.
Just before serving, heat sauce and stir in lima sprouts. Mix well and heat through. Stir in bacon.

BEANS IN RED WINE

SERVES 4

1 tbsp. oil
1 clove garlic, chopped
2 tbsp. chopped parsley
1 cup tomatoes
½ cup dry red wine
4 cups sprouted pinto beans, steamed until tender
  salt to taste
  freshly-ground pepper

In large skillet heat oil.
Sauté garlic and parsley for 2 minutes.
Add tomatoes and wine.
Simmer uncovered for 10 minutes.
Stir in bean sprouts and heat through.
Season to taste.

Serve over rice in bowls, with cornbread.

SPANISH BEANS

SERVES 4

4 cups sprouted red kidney beans
1 clove garlic, minced
2 medium onions, sliced
½ cup celery diced
3 tbsp. bacon fat
  salt to taste
  freshly-ground pepper
½ cup strong black coffee
¼ cup Bourbon whiskey
  sour cream

Preheat oven to 350°.
In skillet, heat bacon fat.
Sauté onions, garlic and celery until soft.
Place in 2-quart baking dish with bean sprouts.
Stir in salt, pepper, coffee and Bourbon.
Cover and bake for 1 hour.
Check dish for liquid content during baking. If dry, add coffee.
Serve with sour cream to spoon on top.

129

RANCH SALAD

SERVES 4 – 6

3 cups sprouted kidney beans, steamed for 20 minutes, then dried on paper towels.
1 medium onion, chopped fine
1 clove garlic, minced
½ cup chopped parsley
½ cup celery, chopped
6 tbsp. oil
2 tbsp. vinegar
  salt to taste
  freshly-ground pepper
½ tsp. mustard
½ tsp. sugar

In large bowl toss together the bean sprouts, onion, garlic, parsley and celery.

In small bowl mix together with fork the oil, vinegar, salt, pepper, mustard and sugar. Blend well.

Pour dressing over salad and mix gently.

Let stand several hours before serving.

RADISHES

That very ancient vegetable, the radish, comes in a wide variety of sizes, shapes and colors. Like many vegetables it contains a lot of vitamins and minerals and is comparatively non-fattening. However, the main reason for sprouting radish seeds, either red or black, is to give the tangy, peppery flavor to foods that only the radish can provide when the real thing is scarce and expensive. It doesn't take many sprouted radish seeds to lend bite to a salad or sandwich or to some tired winter vegetable combination. And they sprout easily, which is rewarding for the winter gardener.

METHOD: jar
TIME: 2–3 days
LENGTH: ½–1 inches
YIELD: 1 tbsp. makes 4 tbsp.
NOTE: When the sprouts start to bear leaves, put them in the sun for a few hours to become green.

MELANGE OF VEGETABLES

SERVES 4

1 medium zucchini, cut into rounds
1 cup cooked green beans in 1-inch lengths
1 cup crisply cooked celery in ½-inch lengths
3 tbsp. butter or margarine
  salt to taste
  freshly-ground pepper
2–3 tsp. radish sprouts

Heat butter in skillet or wok and sauté zucchini until just tender.
Add beans, celery, salt and pepper.
Stir all together and heat through.
Just before serving toss with radish sprouts.

CUCUMBER MOUSSE

SERVES 6

2 medium cucumbers
1 tbsp. lemon juice
2 envelopes plain gelatin
¼ cup cold water
  salt to taste
½ tsp. radish sprouts or to taste
1 cup mayonnaise
½ cup heavy cream, whipped

Peel cucumbers, cut in half lengthwise and scrape out seeds.
Cut into chunks, place in bowl.
Cover with boiling water and add lemon juice.
Soak for 15 minutes. Drain well.
Soak gelatin in cold water in small cup.
Set cup in simmering water to melt gelatin until clear.
Place cucumbers in blender and blend for 20 seconds.
Add melted gelatin, salt, radish sprouts and mayonnaise.
Blend 10 seconds.
Turn out into bowl and fold in whipped cream.
Pour into quart mold and chill several hours.
Unmold onto platter and garnish with watercress.
Serve with mayonnaise.

STUFFED RAW
MUSHROOMS

18 medium-sized mushroom caps, unpeeled
1 8 oz. pkg. cream cheese
1 tbsp. chopped chives
1 tbsp. chopped parsley
1 tsp. sprouted radish seeds or to taste

Wipe mushroom caps with paper towel dampened with lemon juice.
Cream together the cheese and herbs.
Blend in sprouts to taste.
Fill mushroom caps and refrigerate.
Serve as salad or hors d'oeuvres.

DANISH SALAD

SERVES 4

1 cup celery, diced
1 cup cucumber, peeled, seeded and diced
1 cup green pepper, diced
½ tsp. radish sprouts
½ cup mayonnaise
½ cup sour cream
1 tbsp. lemon juice
  salt to taste
  freshly-ground pepper

In bowl toss together the celery, cucumber and peppers.
In separate bowl mix with fork the mayonnaise, sour cream, lemon juice,
    salt, pepper and sprouts.
Blend dressing with vegetables and let marinate for an hour.
Serve on fresh greens.

MUSTARD

The tiny mustard seed, with a power that belies its size, has been known since Biblical times for strength as well as flavor. It was a very important spice for improving as well as disguising foods. The mustard seed when sprouted is strong and spicy and bears little or no resemblance to the ball-park mustard we spread lavishly on hot dogs. It must be treated with respect, as a little goes a long way, and just a few sprouts will pick up the most mundane sauces.

METHOD: jar
TIME: 2–3 days
LENGTH: ½–1 inch
YIELD: 1 tbsp. makes 3–4 tbsp.

BLUE CHEESE SPREAD

MAKES APPROX.
1½ CUPS

½ lb. blue cheese
¼ lb. cream cheese
4 tbsp. butter
¼ tsp. mustard sprouts
2 tbsp. brandy
  salt to taste

Soften cheeses and butter.
Put all ingredients in bowl and mix together, blending well.
Refrigerate for 1 hour.
Bring to room temperature before using as a spread or stuffing for celery or
     endive leaves.

SHRIMP PASTE

MAKES 2 CUPS

1 lb. cooked shrimp
4 tbsp. soft butter
  salt to taste
  freshly-ground pepper
2–3 tbsp. mayonnaise
¼ tsp. ground mace
¼–½ tsp. mustard sprouts

Put shrimp through finest blade of meat grinder.
Put in bowl with remaining ingredients.
Mash all together with fork until well blended.
Use as spread on crackers or thin buttered toast.

BROILED TOMATOES

SERVES 4

8 tomato halves, unpeeled
½ cup mayonnaise
2 tbsp. minced onion
2 tbsp. grated Parmesan cheese
¼–½ tsp. mustard sprouts or to taste

In small bowl mix together the mayonnaise, onion, cheese and sprouts.
Arrange tomato halves in single layer on greased baking pan.
Spread each half with mayonnaise mixture.
Broil until tops are puffy and lightly browned.

PIQUANT SAUCE

2 tsp. finely-chopped shallots or green onions
¼ cup dry white wine
4 tbsp. butter
2 tbsp. lemon juice
½ tsp. mustard sprouts or to taste
2 tbsp. chopped parsley

Put shallots and wine in small saucepan.
Bring to a boil and boil hard until liquid is almost evaporated. Watch closely.
Add to pan the remaining ingredients.
Heat all together.
Pour over broiled fish or chicken.

FENUGREEK

Fenugreek is derived from a Latin word that means "Greek hay," but don't let that put you off. The flavor of this sprouted seed is just the opposite of that sweet grain; it is spicy and slightly bitter and *might* be called an "acquired taste." However if you buy a packaged mixture of seeds for sprouting, fenugreek probably will be included among them, and you may want to experiment a bit.

Like many seeds or grains of ancient origin, this one is supposed to have curative powers such as in the treatment of ulcers (far from the bland diet cure) and as a gargle when made into tea. It is rich in iron, high in protein and vitamin A. And if you know that fenugreek is a component of curry powder, and have experienced the throat-searing results of a strong curry dish, its medicinal claims may not seem too far-fetched. But watch it. This one is strong.

METHOD: jar
TIME: 2–3 days
LENGTH: just sprouted
YIELD: ¼ cup makes 3–4 cups

SHRIMP IN CUCUMBERS

SERVES 4

2 large cucumbers, peeled
½ lb. shrimp, cooked and chopped
3 oz. pkg. cream cheese
½ tsp. curry powder
1 tbsp. fenugreek sprouts or more to taste
   mayonnaise

Cut cucumbers in half lengthwise and crosswise. Scoop out seeds, making "boats."
Sprinkle with salt, turn cut side down on plate and drain.
Mix together with the shrimp, cream cheese, curry powder and sprouts.
Add enough mayonnaise to make a soft filling.
Dry cucumbers.
Fill with shrimp mixture and place on beds of salad greens.

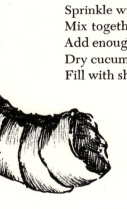

GREEN RICE SALAD

SERVES 4 – 6

3 cups cooked rice
½ cup chopped watercress leaves
½ cup chopped chives
½ cup chopped parsley
   salt to taste
   freshly-ground pepper
¼ cup fenugreek sprouts
½ cup vinaigrette dressing

In large bowl, put all ingredients and toss together until well mixed.
Chill well.

SOURCES FOR SPROUTING SEEDS

THE ORGANIC DIRECTORY, Rodale Press, Emmaus, Penna. 18049. This is source book for all organic food suppliers.

BEALE'S FAMOUS PRODUCTS, Box 323, Ft. Washington, Penna. 19034. Assortment of 15 different seeds in small test packages.

WALNUT ACRES, Penns Creek, Penna. 17862. All kinds of seeds and grains. Interesting free catalogue.

NATURAL DEVELOPMENT CO., Bainbridge, Penna. 17502. Reasonable prices. A large assortment of organically-grown seeds, including bush limas and edible green soybeans.

SHILOH FARMS, Rt. 59, Sulphur Springs, Ark. 72768. Send for catalogue, but they sell mostly wholesale. The only present source for Triticale.

APHRODISIA, 29 Carmine St., N.Y., N.Y. 10014. Fascinating catalogue of some very unusual items.

Your local health food store is a good source for the usual sprouting seeds and grains.

INDEX